About Face

★ ★ ★ ★ ★

Military Resisters
Turn Against War

About Face

★ ★ ★ ★ ★

Military Resisters
Turn Against War

Edited by
Buff Whitman-Bradley
Sarah Lazare
Cynthia Whitman-Bradley

Voices from the
Courage to Resist
Audio Project

About Face: Military Resisters Turn Against War
© 2011 Buff Whitman-Bradley, Sarah Lazare, and Cynthia Whitman-Bradley
This edition © 2011 PM Press

ISBN: 978-1-60486-440-3
LCCN: 2011927945

Cover design by John Yates/stealworks.com
Interior design by Jonathan Rowland
Photos by Jeff Paterson
"Free Bradley Manning" poster by Alisha Bermejo

PM Press
PO Box 23912
Oakland, CA 94623
www.pmpress.org

Courage to Resist
484 Lake Park Ave #41
Oakland, CA 94610
www.couragetoresist.org
510-488-3559

Printed on recycled paper by the Employee Owners of Thomson-Shore in Dexter, Michigan.
www.thomsonshore.com

For Mike Searle and Bill Hard
—BWB

For Mom, Dad, Ben, and Kinley
—SL

For my children
—CWB

Contents

★ ★ ★ ★ ★

Part I: Refusing to Go Back

Part II: Rejecting Military Culture

Part III: Looking Deeper

Part IV: Resisting Military Abuse

Part V: Collateral Murder, WikiLeaks, and Bradley Manning

Afterword

Courage to Resist, formed shortly after the U.S. invasion of Iraq in 2003, is a group of concerned community members, veterans, and military families who support members of the U.S. military who decide that they can no longer participate in wars of empire and occupation waged by the U.S. government.

In the past several years, tens of thousands of service members have resisted illegal war and occupation in a number of different ways: by going AWOL, seeking conscientious objector status or a discharge, asserting the right to speak out against injustice from within the military, and, for a relative few, publicly refusing to fight.

Although the efforts of Courage to Resist are primarily focused on supporting public GI resisters, the organization also strives to provide political, emotional, and material support to all military objectors critical of our government's current policies of empire.

With the limited resources of a grassroots, mostly volunteer organization, Courage to Resist has nevertheless been able to provide assistance to a great many resisters, including those in this book—publicizing their stories through our website and other media; organizing people all over country to write military and public officials in their behalf; sending them books and personal items; creating national support campaigns; and raising funds for civilian legal representation that has helped many of them stay out of military prison, receive lighter sentences, or avoid dishonorable discharges and loss of veterans' benefits.

Courage to Resist is motivated by a "people power" strategy that we believe can weaken the pillars that maintain war and occupation in Iraq, Afghanistan, and elsewhere. By supporting GI resistance, counterrecruitment, and draft resistance, we hope to diminish the number of troops available for unjust war and occupation.

Preface

The Courage to Resist Audio Project

Some of the most eloquent and powerful voices raised against U.S. wars of imperialist aggression are those of the soldiers who have been called upon to fight and have uttered a resounding *no!* An important part of the work Courage to Resist does in supporting the growth of resistance inside and outside the military is to provide opportunities for the voices of GI resisters to be heard. We have published their personal statements as well as articles about them on our website; we have arranged press conferences and speaking tours; and through our Audio Project we have made it possible to hear many of those courageous resisters telling their own stories.

From 2007 to 2009, the Courage to Resist Audio Project recorded telephone interviews with more than two dozen GI resisters. It was my good fortune to be the member of the Courage to Resist organizing collective who produced the Audio Project and conducted those interviews. Invariably, I finished each conversation with enormous respect and admiration for the speaker at the other end of the line. To a person, they were thoughtful and articulate about the reasons they chose to go AWOL, seek conscientious objector status, or refuse to be recalled, and were very, very brave in confronting the possible consequences—including prison—of their actions.

This book is a compilation of most of the interviews originally posted, and still available, on the Courage to Resist website. In editing them, we have removed the interviewer's questions so that the only voice you "hear" is the resister telling her or his own story. We have also made some other small editorial changes and adjustments as necessary for clarification of facts, eliminating repetition, and smooth transitions between topics. Mostly what you will be reading are the words as they were spoken. I believe that you will find them compelling, often disturbing, and making a powerful argument against the arrogant cruelty of militarism and empire.

Please note that at the time of this writing, the legal circumstances of some of the resisters in this book, particularly those in Canada, were unresolved. That may have changed in the intervening time between completion of the manuscript and when you are reading this.

The editors would like to thank the brave resisters who tell their stories in these pages, and current and past members of the Courage to Resist organizing collective—Jeff Paterson, Lori Hurlebaus, David Solnit, Marissa Diorio, Ayesha Gill, Sara Rich, Margaret Howe, Bob Meola, Michael Thurman, and Melissa Roberts (along with the three editors of this book)—for their continuing support for the Audio Project and this book. In addition, we wish to thank David M. Gross, Maria Abad, and Sarah Arid for their tireless work transcribing the interviews that comprise the bulk of this book, and to former Courage to Resist office manager and collective member Adam Seibert for persisting in the search to find these volunteer transcribers.

—*Buff Whitman-Bradley*

Commonly used acronyms and terms

AIT   Advanced Individual Training, which occurs after Basic Training

AWOL   absent without leave

IED   improvised explosive device

IP   Iraqi police

IRR   Individual Ready Reserve; IRR soldiers have completed active duty but may be recalled to service

MP   military police

NCO   noncommissioned officer

PFC   private first class, a military rank held by junior enlisted persons

PT   physical training

PTSD   post-traumatic stress disorder

Stop-Loss   involuntary extension of active-duty service under the enlistment

VA   United States Department of Veterans Affairs, formerly the Veterans Administration

How can there be GI resistance with no draft? Why would someone who voluntarily signed up to serve in the military refuse to fight? There is a common perception that war resistance is something that happens when civilians are drafted into the military and nonconsensually sent off to fight for their country. Yet, as the wars in Iraq and Afghanistan drag on year after year, we are seeing widespread resistance coming from within the ranks of our "all-volunteer" military.

The truth is that GI resistance is happening not despite a so-called all-volunteer fighting force but because of it. In order to understand this, two false assumptions must be dispelled: the assumption that recruits are not coerced into today's military; and that those who sign up voluntarily, even eagerly, cannot change their minds and decide to take a stand against the war.

Not infrequently, people who are initially the most gung-ho about the war become the most deeply disillusioned once they experience the reality on the ground. Contrary to popular perception, during the Vietnam War, the most GI resistance came not from the ranks of draftees but from those who had willingly signed up. And today, many who enlist believing in the righteousness of the wars in Iraq and Afghanistan change their minds once they experience the horror of being an occupier, build relationships with Iraqis and Afghans, or gain firsthand experience of the disconnect between the U.S. government's story about the wars and what is actually happening. Soldiers speak of having their preconceptions about the war shattered by their experience in the military, leaving them confused, angry, and defiant toward what's been hammered into them from the moment they arrived at boot camp.

It is also important to note that many in the military did not sign up enthusiastically, but were coerced or manipulated into service through economic circumstances or aggressive military recruiting. The military spends billions of dollars annually to target and recruit youth by entering schools, instating junior ROTC [Reserve Officers' Training Corps] programs and allowing people as young as seventeen years old to enlist. Studies have shown that the military disproportionately targets youth of color to fill its ranks, and recruiters promise citizenship to undocumented youth if they are willing to join. In a society where youth of color are highly criminalized and surveyed, many see joining the military as an alternative to jail or deportation.

Recruits are promised a ticket out of poverty and routinely lied to about what their tours will look like, often being told that they can opt out of being sent to war. As the economy slumps and the military scrambles to fill a fighting force exhausted and overextended by endless wars and occupations, this coercion is only becoming more intense. These realities set the stage for GI resistance in today's military. The ranks are filled with people who are angry and disillusioned by what they have been made to do for a war they never believed in but only signed up to fight so that they could climb out of poverty. The military rarely delivers on its promise to pull troops out of poverty, or even to take care of them adequately when they return from war with deep mental and physical wounds.

Whether it is because of a growing awareness that the wars and occupations in Iraq and Afghanistan are brutal and unjust, or disillusionment with the military's failure to deliver on its promises, or some combination of these and other reasons, GI resistance within our "all-volunteer" military is alive and well. According to the Associated Press, U.S. Army soldiers are refusing to serve at the highest rate since 1980, with an 80 percent increase in desertions since the invasion of Iraq in 2003. Over 150 GIs have publicly refused service and spoken out against the wars, all risking prison and some serving long sentences. An estimated 250 U.S. war resisters are currently taking refuge in Canada. Countless others leave quietly, disappearing from the ranks, unrecorded by the military.

The stories in this book cast light on the nuanced and varied reasons people in today's U.S. military decide to resist service. Soldiers tell of the military abuse, racism, sexual harassment, assault, rape, and inadequate mental or physical healthcare that are endemic to the U.S. military. They tell of how they couldn't survive another deployment, having already faced two, three, or four, in an exhausted and overextended fighting force. Some tell of resisting because of what they witnessed or were made to do in wars and occupations defined by high civilian death tolls and constant indigenous insurgency. They tell of being targeted by recruiters because they were low-income, had no money for going to college, and no other future prospects.

Perhaps what comes through most clearly in all of these stories is the interaction of personal conscience and courage with the grim circumstances of today's wars and military. The resisters in this book have their own unique life histories and experiences of war and military life. They have all transformed into powerful and courageous agents of change in the face of these histories and conditions. Their voices and narratives help us understand what these processes of transformation look like in today's military. These stories remind civilians who are working against today's wars that supporting GI resistance is a powerful and relevant antiwar strategy as well as a highly personal process of change and growth.

—*Sarah Lazare*

Resistance to Wars of Empire
An Interview with Noam Chomsky

Noam Chomsky is a preeminent linguist, social critic, political theorist, and activist. He has written extensively about U.S. war and empire, imposed through militarism as well as coercive economic institutions, such as the World Bank and International Monetary Fund. In this interview, Chomsky looks at the U.S.-led wars in Iraq and Afghanistan and the potential of GI resistance to play a role in bringing the troops home.

Sarah Lazare: First of all, what do you think about U.S. troops who refuse to fight in Iraq and Afghanistan? Do you think this is a cause worthy of support?

Noam Chomsky: Well, I would support it. I don't think people ought to take part in criminal actions. An aggressive war is a criminal action. Of course there are conflicting motives and reasons. I don't feel entitled to pass judgment on individuals, but those who refuse to participate in a criminal action for principled reasons, yes, they should be supported, I think.

SL: Can you say more about why you consider the wars in Iraq and Afghanistan to be criminal actions?

NC: I mean, they are *prima facie* wars of aggression. The war in Afghanistan was unleashed with an official goal, not what's later claimed. When Bush started bombing Afghanistan he had informed the Afghan people: you're going to be bombed until the Taliban hand over to us someone who we suspect of involvement in a crime against us. The crucial word is "suspect." They had no evidence. Eight months later, the FBI recognized that they still had no evidence. They only had beliefs. They believed that the plot might have been hatched in Afghanistan. So they certainly had no evidence when they started bombing. The Taliban had in fact offered to discuss extradition. We don't know how sincere they were, but they made the offer. But they asked for evidence. Well, that's normal. You don't extradite someone without evidence. But the Bush administration, and in fact the West generally, regarded that as an outrageous demand. How can you ask evidence from us if we want to do something? So they provided no evidence and then they bombed. There was no authorization from the Security Council. It's common to appeal to a later resolution. First of all, it was later, and secondly it doesn't authorize it.

So yes, it was a criminal act, and it was undertaken, we should remember, with the expectation that it might have really dire effects. The expectation on the part of the government, reported in the press, specialists on Afghanistan, the aid agencies, was that the bombing might lead to the death of millions of people. Since the country was on the verge of starvation, even the threat of bombing had driven the aid agencies out. The numbers used in the press were maybe two-and-a-half million people might be driven over the edge of starvation. Well, fortunately, the worst didn't happen, but that doesn't matter. When you evaluate an action, you ask about the circumstances at the time, not the outcome.

So, sure, it was a criminal act by any measure. It was also bitterly denounced by many of the leading anti-Taliban resisters. The U.S. favorite, Abdul Haq, who was later killed when the CIA wouldn't rescue him, was a leading member of the Afghan resistance. He bitterly condemned the bombing. He said, you're bombing just to show off your muscle and you're undermining the efforts of people like those of us who are trying to overthrow the Taliban from within, and he had plenty of support in that. So yes, I think it was a criminal act and remains so.

The invasion of Iraq is not even worth a discussion. This, of course, is criminal aggression. So there was no other pretense. I mean there's a pretense about weapons of mass destruction and links to al-Qaeda. In fact, we know now that the Bush administration was so intent and desperate to find evidence that they resorted to torture to try to elicit confessions that would establish the link that they wanted to justify the invasion. Not that it would have justified it, but they couldn't establish the link so they invaded anyway. Later stories were concocted about bringing democracy and so on, but those are afterthoughts and it would be irrelevant anyhow. So sure, they're criminal enterprises, and in the case of Iraq, it's devastated the country and there are hundreds of thousands, maybe a million dead, several million people displaced, several million exiles, a large part of the country destroyed. Iraqis commonly compare it to the Mongol invasions in the thirteenth century. So, sure, refusing to participate in that is a very legitimate act.

SL: What do you think were the real motives behind these criminal acts of aggression?

NC: Well, in the case of Iraq it's pretty transparent. Iraq has probably the second largest energy reserves in the world. It's right at the heart of the world's major energy-producing regions. The U.S. clearly intended to establish a client regime in Iraq with huge military bases all over the country, which were being built, in fact they're still being built, essentially to establish itself in a position to extend its domination of the world's major energy resources. Now it didn't turn out exactly the way they wanted, thanks to very substantial Iraqi resistance, nonviolent resistance, incidentally. The Bush administration was compelled to back down step by step from its initial goals. It was compelled to permit elections, which it didn't want. It tried to manipulate them but that failed. Just over a year ago, the official position of the Bush administration was that any outcome had to allow unlimited U.S. troop presence and must privilege U.S. corporations in investing in the oil system. Well, they had to back down on that, too, to some extent. We don't know how it will work out, but at least on paper they had to back down a lot. But the aims were pretty obvious to anyone with their eyes open. There are people who claim the U.S. would have invaded even if Iraq's main export was asparagus and tomatoes and the energy system in the world was in the South Pacific, but that's just too irrational to discuss. In the case of Afghanistan, it may have been what Abdul Haq, the anti-Taliban leader said, that it's a way to show your muscle.

SL: How do you think the current economic crisis in the United States is going to impact the ability of the U.S. to wage wars like these in the future or to continue these wars?

NC: Well, you know, nobody exactly knows how the economic crisis is going to resolve itself. But first of all, the economic crisis has not affected the military system. That's kind of fixed, in fact it's expanding. So military producers right now, if you read the business press, they're quite excited about the new opportunities for profit from the expanded government investment in military systems and new planning and so on.

Will the U.S. economy be able to sustain it? That's uncertain, it depends how the financial and manufacturing crises play out. It's not unlikely that the U.S. will emerge from this in a stronger position than its major competitor, which is Europe. It's certainly a blow to the population and the economic system, but it's not clear how serious a blow it is. There's no indication now at least that the outcome will significantly affect the U.S. ability to carry out aggressive war. And it's planning to. It's laying the basis for that.

Just a few days ago, it was announced that the U.S. is building a mega-embassy in Pakistan, kind of like the one they built in Baghdad. It's like a city within a city, not an embassy in any serious sense. They're now building one in Islamabad with side monstrosities in several other cities, Lahore and Peshawar, and apparently they're planning to do the same in Kabul, just as they had in Iraq. Those are signals of an intention to have a massive presence in these strategically and economically crucial areas. The U.S. continues to pre-position military equipment in countries around the region. In fact, it was sending arms to Israel right in the middle of the attack on Gaza for pre-positioning. There's no indication that the huge array of military bases is going to be closed down except for tactical reasons. So the basis for large-scale intervention is being sustained.

SL: What are some strategies that you think the peace movement should be embracing for ending the wars in Iraq and Afghanistan, and how do you see GI resistance fitting into these strategies?

NC: Well, the core issue is always education. You can't have successful activism without a public that understands what you are doing. That's the tactical lesson that activists have to internalize and grasp. So, what I've just been saying is far from common understanding. In fact, you can't even find a word to this effect practically in mainstream discussion.

Take for example President Obama. He's praised by liberals, by much of the left for what's called his principled opposition to the war in Iraq from the very beginning. Well, what was his principled opposition? He said he thought it was a strategic blunder. You could have read that in *Pravda* in the early 1980s about the Russian war in Afghanistan: it's a strategic blunder. In fact, the German General Staff during the Second World War after Stalingrad doubtless criticized Hitler's two-front war as a strategic blunder. We don't call that principled opposition. Principled opposition would mean it's wrong whether it succeeds or not. In fact, many commentators now say: well, you know, Bush was really right, the surge succeeded. Whether it did or not is a separate question, but the debate is interesting. It's like saying Putin should be praised because his devastation of Chechnya succeeded. In fact, Chechnya is now rebuilding; the city of Grozny, which was leveled, is now a booming city. There's construction all over. They have electricity; there are very few Russian troops around; it's run by Chechens; it's wonderful. We don't say that. But in our case, we cannot bring ourselves to accept elementary moral considerations that we readily accept for others. The U.S. is not unique in that. It's quite standard for major powers. You can apply standards to others, but not to yourself. And until there is a willingness to apply to ourselves the proper standards, the kinds we routinely apply to others, activism is going to have to adjust itself to whatever level of understanding has been achieved, and you can try to carry out acts that will raise the level of understanding. It's here that the GI resistance plays quite a significant role, just as it did in the Vietnam War. It's a kind of testimony that can't be written off as crazy students or psychotic leftists, and it has to be faced. They're in a strong position to say what it's like, what we're doing, why it's wrong, and so on, and that's incredible testimony. So, yes, they can play a central role in developing the general understanding that we really should learn how to look into the mirror and apply to ourselves the proper standards, the ones we apply routinely to others.

SL: What do you see as some of the biggest challenges that the peace and antiwar movement faces now that Barack Obama is president?

NC: Well, Barack Obama has energized a lot of people. He's created a great sense of hopefulness, and in my view, these are illusions. I suspect that his policies, I had assumed in advance, it's becoming more and more clear right now, that his policies would be pretty much those of the second Bush administration, not the first one which was kind of off the spectrum, but the second one. But prettified, more pleasant rhetoric, kind of a nice tone, and so on, and the peace movement's going to have to adjust to that. There's an understandable but highly misguided attempt to try to give an interpretation to what he does that's favorable to our own aims, but has no basis in fact. Maybe it's an expression of hope, but sooner or later, and I'd hope sooner, the facts should be faced without illusion. To the extent that Obama's considering continuing what are criminal policies both domestically and internationally, well, yes that should be confronted without any escape hatch, like, well he's really trying but he can't do it because of Congress or something like that. Let's face the reality. So when he expands the wars in what's now called AfPak, okay, we should face that he's expanding them because he wants to expand them. He's not being forced into it. When his administration undermines the prospects for a single-payer health plan, which is what the majority of the population wants, as it is in fact now doing, we should face that and say, okay, that's what he is. He never pretended to be anything different, and don't be misguided by illusions and hopes and expectations. Now it's harder to do, and the same with, say, things like torture, detention without charge, and so on. The Obama administration is slowly trying to reinstitute many of the major Bush programs. Okay, that should be faced for what it is. Mainly, they had no principled objection. They just didn't like the way they were carried out; they were rhetorically harmful and so on. Those were all challenges to overcome.

SL: Thank you very much for this interview. It really helps our movement and is a great way to support resisters who are risking themselves.

NC: Yes, hope it helps. I'm glad to see what you're doing.

—*Sarah Lazare*

Part I:
Refusing to Go Back

★ ★ ★ ★ ★

There are many within the ranks of the U.S. military who refuse to fight because of what they have witnessed and perpetrated in combat. In wars replete with atrocities and high civilian death counts, direct experience often compels soldiers to put down their weapons and refuse to serve. This section will highlight the voices of troops who, after serving in a war zone, said, "Enough!"

After years of war in Afghanistan and Iraq, we have seen the grim realities of these U.S.-led occupations only worsen. The resistance grows as the occupations continue, and the U.S. government uses this ever-intensifying opposition as justification for further force and aggression. With thirty thousand more troops being sent to Afghanistan and bombs raining down on neighboring countries, U.S. troops find themselves in the position of enforcing occupation on an unconsenting population through coercion, violence, and constant surveillance. So-called counterinsurgency strategies amount to nothing more than scorched-earth policies rooted in razing homes, conducting night raids, and engaging in deadly special operations strikes.

The on-the-ground realities for occupying troops are chilling. Soldiers—some fresh out of boot camp, some facing their fourth or fifth deployment—are made to play the role of occupiers, roaming the streets with tanks and weapons, imposing curfews on civilian populations, raiding homes in the middle of the night, and falling victim to roadside bomb explosions and shootings.

These wars have been characterized by multiple and lengthy deployments for U.S. troops who are already overextended from fighting two wars. Many of those now being sent to Afghanistan have already served multiple deployments in the so-called "War on Terror." By 2008, approximately one-third of service members had served two tours in Iraq or Afghanistan, and one-tenth had served three tours. Today, more than eleven thousand U.S. troops have served six tours.

The high rates of post-traumatic stress disorder (PTSD) and depression among those who serve in these wars illustrate the ways in which trauma brutalizes the occupier as well as the occupied. According to a study by the Rand Corporation, rates of PTSD and traumatic brain injury among troops deployed to Iraq and Afghanistan have been disproportionately high, with a third of returning troops reporting mental problems and 18.5 percent of all returning service members battling either PTSD or depression. Each tour greatly increases a service member's chances of developing PTSD. Almost 30 percent of troops on their third deployment suffer from serious mental-health problems, and veterans with PTSD are six times more likely to attempt suicide.

Marine suicides doubled between 2006 and 2007, and Army suicides are at the highest rate since records were first kept in 1980. According to a Congressional Quarterly compilation in November 2009, 334 active-duty military service men and women took their own lives in 2009. As this does not include veterans who have been discharged from the military, the real numbers are probably far higher.

The refusal to fight of those who have already served in combat shows that anyone can change. Many who have been the paid arms of the state in an unjust war of occupation have transformed themselves into peace activists, and in so doing continue to undermine the war that depends on their consent. These repeated transformations, in conjunction with resistance from the people who are being occupied, have the power to end unjust war and uproot occupation.

These refusals also point to the limits of what the U.S. government can ask the military to do. The human mind and body can only take so much. The U.S. government cannot ask troops to sacrifice indefinitely. Eventually, the government will come up against the limits of what troops are able or willing to give. As these wars and occupations continue, it seems likely that more and more resistance will come from within the ranks.

Benji Lewis

October 2008

Benjamin "Benji" Lewis was honorably discharged from the Marines after two deployments to Iraq. Subsequent to his discharge, Benji was notified that the Marines were considering recalling him to active duty. On October 18, 2008, at a Winter Soldier event in Portland, Oregon, he announced his intention to refuse to return to the Marines.

I joined the Marine Corps, actually, as soon as I turned seventeen, and about six months after that I got my high-school diploma and went to boot camp. That was in 2003. I was going through kind of a rough spell in my life, kind of seeking direction. I felt at that time that the military was my chance to do some good and help out in the world.

I went to boot camp in San Diego and I was there for about four to six months before my first deployment to Iraq in 2004. Initially, we were sent to Okinawa. We were told we weren't going to Iraq. But once we got to Okinawa, we were notified that we were deploying to Iraq. At that time, my name came up because of testing scores and my ASVAB [Armed Forces Vocational Aptitude Battery]. I had a 99 on my ASVAB and 134 GT [General Technical] and they took me back to California, to Twentynine Palms, for Arabic language training. I was being trained to be a quasi-interpreter.

Haditha and Fallujah

When I returned to my unit, we went to Iraq. We were stationed at the Haditha Dam and we were running patrols in and around the city of Haditha and starting to build a rapport with the police department there. In March or April, we demobilized from the Haditha Dam and we went to assist in the push through Fallujah. While I was in Fallujah, I was also the adjusting "A" gunner for my mortar platoon, and we spent about two weeks or so lobbing mortars at Fallujah and then we maintained a presence there for another two weeks to a month before we went back to Haditha.

Once we were in Haditha again, my platoon was split basically into two provisional rifle platoons. Because of my language skills, I was attached to the one that was stationed in the Haditha police department where we stayed for a couple of months, basically guarding the police, the police station, while other units of the Marine Corps were to help aid the police in taking over security of their own town.

The closest I got to going into Fallujah was after we had basically pulverized the town. Artillery and air strikes were pretty much just pulverizing the town. Then our unit pushed in and we operated as a close frontline support for the riflemen as they were going street to street. They took three streets, and the rules of engagement would change and they'd fall back and then they'd go back and we kept up that mess for a week or two. Then the command post was formed at the edge of the city of Fallujah, and it was actually pretty much a dump site, you know, trash and garbage everywhere where they set up the command post. We maintained an active mortar posture there and stood guard, but by that time pretty much all the action had died down and most of the resistance elements in Fallujah had fled.

No Chance to Reflect

Actually it wasn't until significantly later, after my second tour, that I was able to start reflecting. We didn't get a whole lot of sleep in Iraq and because I was the adjusting "A" gunner for my entire mortar platoon, I got even less sleep because I always had to be by the gun, manning the gun. When we went to the Haditha police department, our guard rotation was such that we were lucky to get three hours of sleep or so a night. I would say I was pretty much sleep-deprived for the majority of my Marine Corps experience. The time for reflection, we didn't really do it; we didn't talk about it; we didn't want to talk about it so much. We were just looking forward to mail call. We were looking forward to the next time we'd get to go to the PX [Post Exchange] and buy some distractions or pick up some books or whatever. So I'd say for the most part, I never really reflected on what we were doing at that time.

At the time of the battle of Fallujah, we were told we were going in to fight the resistance fighters who had hung the four U.S. contractors on the bridge leading into Fallujah. Much later, I learned that killing them was in retaliation for a U.S.-endorsed assassination by Israel of a quadriplegic Muslim cleric. That was when I started really thinking back to my Marine Corps experience and realizing that most of what I was being told by my commanders was probably not the facts.

The Time between Deployments

I was in Iraq for approximately five months on my first deployment. I came back toward the end of 2004 and from there we had our decompression, went on leave, you know, and I'll be honest with you, it's all really fuzzy because the whole thing kind of ran together, but we had another approximately four or five months of training back in the States before we redeployed to Iraq again.

At that time, I would say that I and most of my fellows pretty much just self-medicated and when we weren't PTing [physical training], when we weren't training, when we weren't in the field, we pretty much stayed in a constant state of drunkenness.

Second Deployment

My second deployment to Iraq in 2005 for OIF 3 [Operation Iraqi Freedom] was, once again, to Fallujah. At this point, through involuntary response or whatever, I'd completely neglected my language and I'd forgotten most of the Arabic I'd learned.

We were stationed at a checkpoint for vehicles leaving and coming into Fallujah. It was about a seven-month deployment and it was a very long and stagnant tour. Not a lot happened. We were kind of just there to be a presence. We'd have eight-, ten-hour days out on the line, where we're wearing all our gear and it was just really hot and we would search vehicles for weapons coming into Fallujah. The whole thing was really ludicrous because there were so many other avenues of smuggling into Fallujah. Why anyone with any armaments would voluntarily go through a vehicle checkpoint, I don't know, but I think for the most part we were getting together a database, and they were issuing all the Fallujah citizens IDs. I think the real purpose of the deployment was just to have an intimidating military posture there.

Good Relationships with Iraqis

I had a lot of respect for the Iraqi citizens, especially after my first tour where I really worked with translators and whoever I could and I tried to speak with them as much as possible. I lived hand-in-hand with them in the Haditha police department. We'd sit post together and we'd talk, we'd try to learn each other's language, teach each other games, you know, pass the time. Most of them, I felt like they were kind of kids just like me and everyone else, kind of caught up in the whole thing and looking for a paycheck and, you know, not really understanding the consequences of the bigger picture.

One story comes to mind. While we were operating the personnel checkpoint, people were going in and getting issued IDs, so they could go into town. These people had been waiting since four or five in the morning to try to get into the city. Well, it was coming toward five o'clock at night and they're closing down the checkpoint and there are still several people in line and we're having to tell them to get going, we're sorry, we can't help you, come back tomorrow. One Iraqi kind of stood up and was like, "Hey, I want to go home," and we were like, "Well, yeah, buddy, we want to go home, too." He was like, "Well, why don't you go home and then after you go home, I can go home," and it was probably the most sensible statement I ever heard the entire war.

Another time a dump truck was driving into the checkpoint. I believe there were three occupants of the vehicle, but I only remember an adult male and a little boy. We found out later that their brake lines had gone out so they couldn't stop at the checkpoint. They were barreling through and we fired a couple of warning shots and then the machine gunner started firing at the engine block with a 240. At that point all the Iraqi guardsmen that we were working with were firing in the air, firing all over the place, and so pretty much it was a duck-and-cover scene for me. Luckily no one was hurt. The dump truck was all shot up, but the little boy and his father were all right.

Back in Twentynine Palms

After seven months we went home on leave and when I came back, I had the opportunity to get out of my unit and get attached to a unit that was called Mojave Viper. It was in Mojave Viper that I spent my last year of in the Marine Corps, as an instructor teaching escalation of force, vehicle checkpoints. I kind of tried to sway the classroom to teach people how they could not discharge their weapons.

After six months, they were going to send me back to my unit and I requested to stay in Mojave Viper because I felt I was doing more good there than I could have been doing back in my unit. The Mojave Viper training wasn't easy. We were pretty much out in the field anywhere from eight to fifteen hours a day, and, in all honesty, that whole year felt like I was still deployed to Iraq. The stress levels for the instructors were pretty high there, even though we were back in the States, because of the numbers of Marines we were training and the intensity of what we were teaching them.

It was during this time that I started reflecting and remembering some of the things I'd witnessed in Iraq. I think one of the most heart-wrenching experiences was in Fallujah, during the push back in 2004. I remember when we heard some M-16 shots going off and kind of looking around going, "What the fuck is going on?" I hear my name getting called and I'm running up there. They were shooting at this lady who was walking up to our posts waving her arms and asking for help in Arabic. So I came up close and talked to her, and her face looked like death itself. She had salt crusted all over her face. It was obvious that she had been crying for quite a bit. I kind of got the story that she had a family. We were like, "Go back home, go to your family." And then it came out that she was asking for help. Three days ago, her entire family, her children, had been pretty much buried in the rubble of their house, and she was asking for help. I asked my staff sergeant, "Can we help her? Can we help her?" He said to tell her to walk to the Red Cross aid station, which was a few miles away. We couldn't leave our posts to help her, so we gave her a couple of bottles of water and wished her luck, you know. It dawned on me later on that me being the adjusting gunner for the mortar section, there was good probability that I was the one that put those rounds on her house.

It was at that time, too, that I was starting to realize all the propaganda that led me to joining the Marine Corps from a very, very young age. I started thinking about all the movies I used to watch, looking at these heroes in these war movies, Clint Eastwood, *Heartbreak Ridge*, *Top Gun*, all these stories that I grew up idolizing. I started realizing that American society was heavily, heavily indoctrinated, and it starts as soon as you can receive messages from television.

Discharged and Called Back

I got out of the Marines in February 2007, pretty much right after I got out of the Marine Corps. I attended spring semester at Mt. San Antonio Community College. When I got my call to report for IRR I determined I wasn't going back in, that I was going to show up, to report, but only to inform them that I wasn't coming back.

Benji Lewis refused orders for his Individual Ready Reserve recall, and was discharged from the military with no penalties.

<u>Samantha Schutz</u>

June 2009

Samantha Schutz's recruiter told her not to say anything to the Army about her past depression and emotional problems, but almost immediately after she started Basic Training, those problems recurred. Samantha sought help and support from the Army and received none. Her emotional difficulties continued through Advanced Individual Training (AIT) and her deployment to Iraq where she worked as an Army journalist. What she did and experienced in Iraq deepened her opposition to a war she had never believed in. Returning to the U.S. on leave, Samantha decided to go AWOL rather than go back to the Middle East.

At the time I joined the Army in 2006, I was going through a lot. In April of that year, I'd been in an inpatient program in my local hospital for a deep depression and kind of an inability to cope with society. I was having a lot of financial trouble and my dream was really just to kind of go on the road. It sounds silly, but my biggest dream was to work odd jobs and sow love and poetry all over America. And my family was telling me that was impossible and I needed to grow up and get a real job and get myself planted and rooted.

When I did sign up, I was nineteen years old and breaking my third lease and had just come out of the hospital and was very mistrustful of authority. I had little to no options and joining was one of the only opportunities that I was be able to find to get money together and make my family trust that I could be an active member of society, even though it wasn't what I wanted.

I really feel that the advertising on TV hooks young people. Like I was into thinking that the Army is not a war machine, it's just a place to get money for college, to better yourself. And I kind of had a naïve take on it all that I think so many people do.

Depression Returns in Basic Training

Just the first week, I was experiencing a lot of the same deep depression I dealt with for about five years solid before I went into the military. I was farther away from my support group and my therapist than I'd ever been, and having just a phone call once a week for support and it was really a shock to my system.

I saw a counselor, well, I think, two times and the first time I was basically told that I had already made a commitment to the Army and my feelings at this point were just something that I needed to get over and I needed to push forward. I know they were just trying to motivate me, but I did not feel that my best interests were being looked out for.

I felt very alone. So the next time I could, I called my grandmother and asked her to have some of my medical records sent from my therapist and from the week that I spent as an inpatient. Even though those records were faxed to the counselors, the counselor told me at our next meeting that it was not an option for me to use that as a way out. The way she put it to me was, "How am I supposed to believe that this is true if you lied just to get into the military?" It was hurtful to me because I knew that the recruiter had told me not to put that stuff on the application. It should have been a red flag to me, but I believed that I was in such a vulnerable state that I pushed forward.

Making It through Basic

I also was dealing with a pelvic injury that I got the first week of Basic and was on and off of crutches and so I was disheartened through that. I didn't know if I was going to be "recycled," as they say, having to repeat Basic all over again. That was my biggest fear. I thought if I could just make it through that maybe it would be easier to find a way to get help or to get out when I made it to AIT.

I did make it through Basic. I gave it all I had. I am proud of myself for pushing through that. Then for AIT, I went to the Defense Information School to learn how to be a print journalist. The training was fourteen weeks. However, I was held over there because I was unable to pass the physical test due to the pelvic injury that was still following me from Basic. That kind of made it worse.

After AIT, I went on to Fort Hood, Texas. I wrote a lot of articles about promotions and what was going on at the base and similar articles about safety and things like that. We used to submit our articles to the two civilian newspapers that were near the base.

Going AWOL to Avoid Iraq

While I was still at Fort Hood, I was really kind of just feeling jaded about seeking help, feeling like no one was on my side and

I needed to take a stand for myself. I didn't want to go to Iraq and when my unit started talking about that it felt like the pressure was really on me and I decided in September of 2007 to go AWOL.

I went on leave from Fort Hood, came to Indiana to my home and didn't go back. Unfortunately, I wasn't aware of how many resources were out there. I felt, at the time, very alone. Some of my friends and some of my family were supportive. Other people were not and I still wasn't very sure of myself or what I could do. So, I was still communicating with my superiors in my unit. We had a lot of phone conversations in which I was very expressive of my feelings and my commander of my... I don't know what it was called... my section commander, he assured me, promised even, that if I came back, he would personally help me seek a discharge.

I believed him, and I went back to Fort Hood after a week of being AWOL. All that really happened was my being AWOL was swept under the rug. They subtracted seven days from my accrued leave, and no one ever talked about it. I did not get punished. I did get to have a conversation with the First Sergeant of my unit in which I was very frank about everything I had been feeling. He again reinforced that I had made a commitment and my feelings did not matter. What mattered was honoring the contract that I had signed.

I felt defeated. Looking back, I wish now that I'd been more aware of the resources that I'd had to help me, and now I'm glad that I've learned to be a stronger person in really asserting my beliefs about things. But I allowed the situation to make me feel defeated, so I just kept going through the motions and the next thing I knew I was waking up on a plane to Iraq—to Kuwait and then to Iraq.

A Military Journalist in Iraq

My mission there was basically the same as at Fort Hood, except that now we had our own publication. However, I did not feel that I was a journalist. I felt like I was a propagandist. It was drilled into all of our heads that we were to put a positive spin on everything and there were only certain things that we could report on. Another part of our job there was to work with the Western media, to guide them. They would come over and embed to get their stories and in a roundabout way we censored what they were allowed to see, experience, write about, or film.

We would organize what missions they would go out on and we knew in advance what missions were likely to see violence and what missions were goodwill missions or building missions or things like that. We would send the media out on the goodwill missions and not mention the violent ones.

I was at the Division level and I was a female, so I wasn't allowed to go out on many of the more dangerous missions. But I feel that my assignments seemed to be centered on ignoring what was going on, just trying to save face and entertain.

I really had thought, "Oh, I'm going to be a war journalist. I'm going to be covering this event that's history, that's controversial." Come to find out, I always knew the media was a little biased, but reporting the news wasn't anything close to what I did.

I actually brought that to the attention of some of the people, some of my colleagues and superiors. What happened was they moved me, moved my position so I was no longer writing. My function now was to be the editor of our newsletter, our daily newsletter. So my job now was a twelve-hour shift at night when I essentially worked alone and just put together this newsletter. It was a lot of busywork and cut and paste. I think they may have thought I was a danger at that point. Or they may have sensed that I was undermotivated. I was alienated from the rest of the staff, working alone twelve hours a night.

A Troubled Conscience

At that time, I had reconnected with an old friend over the Internet, so it was easing up as far as depression, because I had someone that I could relate to that I was able to talk to about things and get my emotions straight. But I was losing a lot of sleep, I was packing in all these other emotions. I had gone into these neighborhoods in Baghdad and seen the way that people were living and then I'd come back to the American base in the middle of all of that, come back to my air-conditioned nice trailer and my nice bed and TV and my refrigerator and microwave and computer. I could walk a half a mile down to Taco Bell or Burger King, Popeye's, a PX [Post Exchange] the size of a Wal-Mart. I was feeling more depressed and guilty because I felt that the American public was being told that we were helping, we were over there now to help them rebuild and recuperate, and it was stunning to me how much money—$12 billion a month in 2008—was being spent over there. It seemed in my eyes to be going more toward our creature comforts than actually helping.

It was hard for me to deal with already being depressed. I also got to the point where I was being irresponsible with my money because my conscience didn't feel that I deserved that money. It was coming from taxpayers who were having the wool pulled over their eyes. So I felt that by being part of the military organization that I was deceiving the American people and it was horrible.

Home on Leave and AWOL Again

I had sort of known before I took my leave that I might not return. I had kind of prepared myself to make the decision when I got home as to whether I was going to return or not. When I came home on leave, I felt that I had no moral choice in the matter. I could not continue. I needed to end it right where it was. So I stayed in the States. I actually traveled with my current partner. He and I traveled to work out West on an organic farm, and it was a complete one-eighty from what I had been doing. I knew then that it was possible for me to really be happy and to have a life where I was a functioning member of society. I was able to live simply and take care of my finances and still do something that I didn't feel was morally wrong.

After going West, we did a little more traveling around there and traveled back to Indiana. We had actually found out that I'd gotten pregnant. I wanted the best possible care for myself and our family. So I wanted at that point to see about turning myself in and taking accountability and getting it behind me as well. So we came back to Indiana so I could prepare to do that. Then I found out that I had miscarried. This was in September 2008, a year after the first time I had gone AWOL.

So I went through another long emotional period. But I still… I was actually going to Fort Sill, Oklahoma, to try turn myself in. I hadn't done all my research and was kind of going blindly into it until I stopped at a motel for the night and realized, "You know what? I'm trying to fight this battle all by myself and I know that this is not the right time or place to be doing this." Intuitively, I didn't feel right about it.

So I came back home and my partner and I decided to do some more traveling and soul searching: do I even want to go back or do I just want to kind of never face this and live under the radar? And I ultimately decided, no, part of what I want to do is have my voice back and be able to help other people heal from their wounds from the war machine and stand up for themselves, too. So I got the courage, again, to come back and work on turning myself in. I called the GI Rights Hotline before and they recommended me to the lawyer, whom I hired, and the lawyer recommended me to Courage to Resist. So I finally felt that it was the right time and place, that I was going to be supported, that I was doing it for the right reasons, and that I would have more control over the situation.

Facing the Consequences

Right now I know that the range of consequences is anywhere from a discharge, a less than honorable discharge—kind of like, "You're not worth it, we should have let you go a long time ago, you know we're not going to even deal with you," all the way to serving another seven and a half months, but instead of in Iraq, in the brig.

I had already prepared myself for even worse. I can honestly say that I would rather have spent the three years I have left on my contract in a cell than serving the military organization. It's not what I would want for anyone, nor myself, but I am prepared.

Under the conditions of her discharge, Samantha Schutz Reiss was banned from Fort Hood and may not receive veterans' benefits.

André Shepherd
December 2008

André Shepherd is the first Iraq War veteran to seek refugee status in Europe. He served as a helicopter mechanic in the U.S. Army in Iraq and while there began to have serious doubts about the U.S. occupation of that country. In 2007, rather than return to Iraq to participate in a war in which he no longer believed, he went AWOL from his base in Ansbach, Germany. On November 26, 2008, André applied for political asylum, asserting that the war in Iraq had been declared illegal by the German government.

I grew up in Cleveland, Ohio, and I went to college at Kent State University. The problem was, I graduated when the dot-com bubble burst, so while I was trying to search for a job in the computer sciences, which I went to school for, I couldn't get a job. So what I ended up doing was working several jobs—in fast foods, as a courier, a vacuum cleaner salesman for a little bit, stuffing envelopes, things like that—just low-paying jobs, trying to make ends meet.

Mentally, I felt like I not only had let myself down, but I'd let my family down, too, because I had a set goal in life—to complete college, have a house, have a family, and to actually do something that would a) make the world at least a little bit better place and b) show my parents that I can live life on my own. And since it didn't work out that way, it was pretty distressing.

Meeting an Army Recruiter

That's when my life started going through two distinct phases: first, I ended up living in my car—once in 2001 for about six months and the second time in 2003 for about the same period of time. Then, in the summer of 2003, I ran into an Army recruiter in Lakewood, Ohio, and he was telling me about the engagements that they were in, and that they needed people like me to help the peoples of the world free themselves from terrorism and dictators and things like that. For example, he used Saddam Hussein, Osama bin Laden, Kim Jong Il—the poster children for the "Axis of Evil." So he talked to me a little bit about that, then he started talking about the Army benefits, the steady pay, ability to travel, free housing, free medical care that would continue even after I left the service. All I had to do was sign up for a few years and I would have all of these benefits. At the time, I was living in my car so I found that really appealing. After a few months debating whether that was a good idea, I decided to join the service on the twenty-seventh of January in 2004.

I knew that since we were engaged in warfare, since the war on terror was going on and everything, that going into combat would be a possibility. At that time, I didn't have the knowledge that I have now. All I had was pretty much what the mass media was telling me and what the Bush administration was saying. At that time, I still trusted my government and believed that they would actually tell us the truth. So it didn't bother me to be going into warfare at all. I thought that I would be doing a great service to my country and that it would actually put my life on the right path.

Assigned to Germany, Then Iraq

Basic Training was held at Fort Jackson, South Carolina, and after that I went to Fort Eustace for AIT for the Apache Helicopter repair. After that, I was permanently assigned to Katterbach Army Airfield located in Ansbach, Germany.

The unit I was assigned to was already deployed for six months by the time I got there, so once I got there, I was reassigned to join them at Camp Speicher, which is outside of Tikrit in Iraq. I was there from September 2004 to the beginning of February of 2005.

Our main mission there was to make sure that the Apache helicopter continued to fly because without proper maintenance, the birds can't get off the ground. So we were working twelve-hour days, six days a week, maintaining the helicopters. Sometimes we would be on duty, watch the local population come inside and help us build the fences, sandbag our defenses to fortify our hootches, which is where our living area was. And sometimes we would be on guard duty.

Starting to See Things Differently

While I was in Iraq, the first thing that I noticed was when the local population would come into our post. When you liberate a people, they are usually overjoyed to see you. They're happy that you want to help them and they welcome you with open arms. When I would see the Iraqi population in the mornings on my way to work, they didn't look like they were in any way happy to see us. They looked like either they were afraid of me, like I was going to hurt them in any kind of way, or if I turned my back without my weapon they would probably want to kill me. So that started me thinking, "Okay, what's going on here, because I thought that we were supposed to be the good guys, and everybody's looking at me like I'm crazy."

I started talking to the soldiers on the base to try to get to know everyone since they were already down there for half a year. A lot of what they were talking about was that they didn't understand why they were there. For me, this is a really big problem, because I'm the type of person that has to have a clear plan as to what's going on so I can effectively do my job, especially if I'm going to be in a combat zone. It didn't make any sense to me that the soldiers didn't see any type of benefit as to why we were there and what our mission was. So it started me thinking, maybe we might have actually made a mistake. I started wondering, "Okay, why *are* we here? The way it's looking from what I've seen of the people, the people pose no threat to the mainland United States and some things don't seem to make any sense."

So I started to do research. I was on the post and I started to see little inconsistencies in what I was reading, you know, between what the Bush administration was telling everybody and what was actually happening, especially in the run up to the Iraq war, because our media essentially shielded the population from any kind of dissidence from the official line. What I started seeing was that major countries like France and Germany were from the start against the war, how the UN was trying to let the weapons inspectors do their job so they could work out the problem without having any armed conflict, and how the Bush administration was trying to ram things through. That started to bother me because it looked to me like there was some type of other agenda going on besides freeing the Iraqi people from a dictator or trying to find weapons of mass destruction.

The other thing that happened there was with the Battle of Fallujah, where they were saying that it's a really great victory for us in Iraq. The way it was portrayed to us on the military channels was that we had done a great thing by lifting a city that was completely overrun by terrorists and insurgents and everything. But continuing my research, I was seeing some really appalling things, like men who were of fighting age, even if they didn't want to fight, weren't allowed to leave the city. Basically, they were just sitting there defenseless, you know. Caught in the siege with the Marines and Army forces and reports of white phosphorous being used and, you know, just the total destruction that was going on in the city.

Feeling like an Oppressor

When I looked at the Iraqi people and they looked at me kind of like how the French would look at Nazi Germany or any of the people who were overrun by the Romans, it made me wonder just what exactly does this flag on my shoulder mean? Because we're supposed to be the symbol of freedom and hope, so you would expect in most places you went that they would be glad to see you. When they weren't, you start to feel really bad, and I started to realize that we made a pretty major mistake. Because I didn't want to be part of something that is the very opposite of the ideal that we were taught since we were little.

We redeployed back in Kitterbach Army Airfield in 2005 and then I got myself a computer and got connected to the Internet. Because for me the Internet is the world's largest library and, you know, when you're in a foreign country it's very difficult to find an English-language library. So that was the main source for me to have a window into the world and see what's going on.

I started digging through news stories and started finding out all the major lies that were told by the Bush administration. Take for example the Downing Street Memo that was released by the British government talking about how the Bush administration already prepared for this war a year in advance before anybody had resolved the issue of weapons of mass destruction. I read how the CIA reported that there were no WMDs [weapons of mass destruction] and found and watched a video where George Bush was making a joke out of it—while the people in Iraq are suffering and dying, he's sitting there making a joke out of it, trying to find weapons of mass destruction on the stage. I mean, stuff like this is just totally uncalled for.

I was also trying to look through the laws—U.S. law and even international law—because I was reading reports how this war was being condemned internationally. What I found was highly disturbing because there is no formal declaration of war that was set forth by Congress. There wasn't one. So by U.S. Constitution standards, this war is completely illegal. And going through the Geneva Conventions, going through the U.N., what happened at the U.N. and how Germany ruled in 2005 that the war was illegal, and that says a lot when a major Western power sits there and rules that the conflict you are in is illegal.

Taking a Stand

Once I pretty much figured out the truth, that this war was basically nothing but a fraud not only on the American people but on the entire world, I resolved that I would not go on another deployment to Iraq. At that time, there was about a two-year period of reorganization, so that gave me time to think. So the major decisions did not come up until January 2007 when we got the warning order that we would be scheduled to deploy in the summer.

At the time I was told there was actually a problem with too many people in our unit. So they had to make a decision to leave some people behind and send the rest. I was one of the guys picked to stay behind. So I thought everything was okay. Four months later, they informed me that I would have to deploy to Iraq.

This was the moment of truth. I had to make a really big decision—whether or not to go ahead in spite of my conscience or say, "No, I can't do this because it's just totally cruel and I don't want to have an indirect hand in anymore atrocities that are going on in Iraq." I talked to one of my NCOs about it privately and he mentioned conscientious objection. The problem with conscientious objection, though, is that unlike most other countries, America has its regulations that you have to be against every single war that's ever fought. It doesn't matter if it's an offensive war, a defensive war. It doesn't matter. You have to be against every single war. For me that is a virtual impossibility, because if they're overrunning America's shores, of course I'm going to pick up a weapon and help to defend it. So that argument right there would throw the conscientious objection thing right out of the window.

At the same time, I was also doing research on other soldiers that were conscientious objectors. The case of Agustín Aguayo popped up and that one was just crazy, you know, how the military treated him when he didn't want to fight any wars period. The guy went down there without a weapon, I mean he went with a weapon but he didn't load it or anything. He was a combat medic so he would have been under fire, but regardless, he refused to fire a weapon. He didn't want to hurt anybody and the military still wanted to force him a second time to Iraq—in handcuffs—just because they didn't believe that he was a true conscientious objector. So that right there told me that conscientious objection was not the way to go.

That left me with two options: either go to Iraq anyway or walk away from the service, because there's no other option. It's either CO [conscientious objector] status or AWOL or just do what you're told.

So on April 11, I went on leave and I ended up going to southern Germany. During the time that I didn't deploy, I traveled a lot in Germany, so I made a lot of good contacts and we discussed the issues. I made a decision within that two-week period that I would have to walk away from the service rather than either get myself killed or get somebody else killed in a war that was based on a pack of lies.

From AWOL to Asylum Application

Just last week, after exhausting every other option I possibly could, from immigrating to Germany to seeing if there was a way to get a U.S. passport so I could reach America, I decided to try for asylum. This idea came up one year ago because I was in contact with the Military Counseling Network and they actually brought that up as one of the options. But I wanted to wait to do that because I knew that going for asylum in a country that had a significant amount of U.S. soldiers would not be an easy task. But at the same time, Germany is a staunch opponent of the Iraq War.

I've heard some people say that my chances are fifty-fifty. It could go either way, and some have gone as low as 10 percent, because of the political aspect of it, not because of the legal aspect. If I was from any other country, most likely I would get it because the war is sanctioned as illegal by a myriad of countries, and the European Union has changed the laws in the last couple of years saying that soldiers who are forced to participate in a war in which war crimes are being committed are allowed to seek asylum. If I lose, I would most likely have to go to military court.

If I do get asylum, my attorney said that I don't have to lose my citizenship. But I'm quite sure the U.S. will reserve the right to revoke my citizenship based on my action.

Family Is Supportive

I didn't keep a lot of contact with my family in the last year and a half while I was AWOL because I wanted to protect them. With the provisions of the Patriot Act, the big controversy with wiretapping, I did not want my parents to get in any trouble for possibly harboring a fugitive or staying in contact with a fugitive or anything like that. I've gotten in contact with them in the last couple of days and explained the situation to them. They're very worried about what can possibly happen to me. However, they are supportive of me because they understand the situation and they see that I took a stand against the things that are going on.

I have quite a bit of support actually. Right now, my biggest supporters are Military Counseling Network, based in Bammental, Germany; Connection e.V., which is in Offenbach; and the other one that I want to give a shout out to is the Iraq Veterans Against the War, which I have been a proud member of for the last couple of months.

There's quite a big groundswell of support from just everyday people, which I really appreciate. I'm happy that so many people see what's really happening on the geopolitical stage and are willing to come forward and give their two cents on the matter.

In April 2011, André Shepherd's application for asylum was refused by the German government, but no decision had been made about whether or not to deport him. As of this writing, he still resides in Germany.

Bryan Currie

May 2008

> *Bryan Currie joined the U.S. Army in 2004. He trained as*
> *an infantryman and grenadier and was sent to Afghanistan*
> *in late 2006. While he was there, a truck he was driving ran*
> *over an explosive device and Bryan was seriously wounded.*
> *He was treated for his wounds in-country and sent back to*
> *duty. In mid-2007, Bryan returned to Fort Polk, Louisiana,*
> *and sought treatment for PTSD, and his status was changed*
> *to nondeployable. His attempts to get meaningful help were*
> *unsuccessful, and his status was changed once again to*
> *deployable. That's when he decided to go AWOL. In March*
> *of 2009, Bryan turned himself in.*

I was deployed eleven months. I can't remember the exact
month I left. When we got there, it was kind of slow because it
was kind of icy, but when the weather warmed up, it was pretty
heavy at some times. We took mostly injuries, not a whole lot of
U.S. deaths. A lot of friendly Afghan forces were killed in action.
They were fighting alongside of us.

We went on raids looking for people or pulling security
around villages, and trying to find Taliban and stuff. The houses
over there are real awkward. They're made 100 percent out of
mud and sticks. So the doorways are really small. It's very hard

to get in and you never know what's going to happen when you walk into a room. We encountered enemy fighters a couple of times and suppressed the threat. And we did capture a couple of people. We also encountered unarmed civilians. A lot of the villagers did get along with us. But they were real two-faced. They would be your friends one minute, then at night they would turn against you or the next day they would turn against you. They just believed everything they heard, so if we told them positive information, the next day the Taliban came and told them negative information about us versus what we just told them about why they shouldn't be Taliban, then they'd go hating us again. It was kind of like taking one step forward and two steps back every day.

The children in the houses, they were always just scared, but we had interpreters and they always reassured the children that we were there to help them and same with all the families, we were there for help and not to harm them unless they were found out to be Taliban and then we'd probably arrest them. Then we'd pretty much just question them if that was the case.

Injured by a Landmine

We were on a convoy to pick up another soldier who had to go back for emergency dental or something. We went back to pick him up and on the way back, we hit a land mine in the road and it blew up. I was the driver of the truck that day. The gunner in the turret got hit in the face with his weapon that was on the turret, and then collapsed his lung and broke his back and some other stuff.

Me, I got burned, I lost four teeth, broke my jaw, I got shrapnel in my hands, my knees are all swollen. It kind of jolted me forward so I think I've got more long-term back pain, nothing right away but now my back is always sore.

When I was in Afghanistan, health care was pretty good. Where I was at, it was a lot of foreign national doctors—Canadians, English, other countries. So it was a pretty diverse area where the hospital was at. So I had teeth put in, and I was pretty much taken care of. But once I got home, I couldn't sleep and I got diagnosed with PTSD. Then the Army just kind of forgets about you.

Back into Combat

I went back into combat after three weeks. It was almost impossible to get back to the States from over there unless you were missing a limb or something like that. There was no question about trying to get back to the States for something just mental or something like PTSD. I guess they thought my injuries were like 100 percent healed.

I was 110 percent on edge, nervous all the time. Even after I got back, they still would make me drive the Humvees, lead truck in the convoys, even though I had asked not to because I had been blown up. I just had anxiety attacks and stuff. It was pretty hard to deal with afterwards, just hoping it wouldn't happen again. It was pretty bad.

The missions actually got worse after I came back. We started doing more heavy missions where they actually knew they had the Taliban pinpointed.

Back in the States

I talked to a psychiatrist on the base. I didn't feel comfortable talking to her, because she was in the military. She would always try to relate that she had gone through the same stuff, but she'd obviously sat behind a desk the whole deployment. But she would always be like, "I know what you're talking about; I know how you feel." And I got fed up so I asked if I could see another psychiatrist, so they sent me to another one. He was a little bit better, but then he started being a jerk. There's no real way to prescribe medicine for PTSD, I guess. They don't have a cure for it or anything yet, so they would just give you a bag of medicine—literally twenty different types of medicine—and be like, "Here, try one and if it doesn't work try another one, and then if that one doesn't work … and once you find one that works, just stick to it."

Then he would tell me, when I was telling about my feelings about going into crowds of people and not liking being in restaurants anymore and stuff like that, then he would be like, "Oh, well, I think you just need to grow up. You're just acting like a kid."

So that's when I stopped even trying with that, because it wasn't going anywhere. He seemed like a fairly nice guy at first, but then when he started saying that stuff, I actually got hotheaded—I have a really short temper now—I started getting hotheaded with him and I guess I made him mad and he didn't want to schedule appointments anymore. But I didn't really want to talk to him anymore either.

PTSD Symptoms

I really don't like crowds of people. I get kind of nervous if there's somebody behind me or stuff like that. I was real easy-tempered before I joined the Army. But now, after dealing with so many rude people and being around so many bad attitudes all the time and being deployed for that long amount of time, I guess my whole attitude changed and now I get real bad road-rage. I fly off the handle real easy. Somebody says one wrong thing and it's like an argument. Another problem I have is sleeping, nightmares, and stuff like that.

I pretty much gave up with the whole psychiatrist thing and trying to get help for medical reasons. I started going on sick calls because my knees were hurting and stuff, and my back was hurting. They gave me a "cannot deploy" profile for my knees being messed up. I couldn't carry over thirty pounds; I wasn't allowed to wear body armor; I wasn't allowed to carry a weapon or anything. So I wasn't deployable, and they said I might have needed to have surgery. But then after the fact, the news that I had a nondeployable profile made it back to my unit, and my commander was like, "No, he's going," and blah blah blah. All my friends were like, "I'm glad you're finally getting the help you need." But a lot of the leadership was like, "Oh, no, you're faking it" and "I've been on six deployments, why is this affecting you so much all of a sudden?" and blah blah blah. There was harassment and a lot of the senior sergeants and stuff that should have been there and supported me and tried to help me were like, "You're a coward. I can see why you're getting a profile, 'cause you're tired of this job, and it's just ridiculous."

After I got to my unit, I guess somebody knew the doctor that gave me the nondeployable profile and they called him and got him to change his opinion. After he had already made his opinion that I wasn't to deploy, then he changed his opinion and said, "Yeah, he can go."

Decision to Leave

I waited until the two days before my unit was supposed to deploy to Iraq and I just packed all my stuff up in my car and I left.

I have a lawyer who's trying to get me to turn myself back in and try to get discharged. I actually did go to a military base in New York where my unit's headquarters is at and I went up there with my whole family and I did a bunch of press conferences and stuff up there. Then when I got onto the base I really didn't like what they were telling me, about how I'd have to stay there for a year minimum, and I'm not going to get right out of the Army like I think I am, I'm going to have to stay there and all this. So I decided to leave again. I kind of had an anxiety attack. I just didn't want to be there. I didn't want to deal with that all over again. I kind of had the assumption that if I stay, then they're just going to say, "Oh, he's good," and send me straight overseas.

Rethinking the Military

I'm pretty much 100 percent against the military now. My brother, he was in, and he's still very for it and he wants to go back. He's out now, but he wants to go back in and to go back overseas. He always says, "You're wrong for being against the military," but I think the military is … I think it's crap. And I don't think we should be in Iraq and Afghanistan. I've probably done a complete U-turn.

Bryan Currie received an honorable discharge in September 2009.

David Cortelyou

April 2008

> *Feeling like he was getting nowhere in searching for jobs, David Cortelyou joined the Army when he was eighteen years old. He was sent to Germany after Basic Training and from there his unit was deployed to Iraq in December 2005. David's experiences in Iraq resulted in severe PTSD. Back in Germany, he went AWOL on two different occasions and was finally released from the Army in the first week of April 2008.*

The first five months in Iraq, we were in Bi'aj—relatively safe and quiet. We had daily mortars and that was about it. The one time a guy tried to lay an IED, he blew himself up. I didn't see it happen, but I saw the after effects. There were chunks of his bones plastered to the wall, so that was not a pretty sight. But, because the guy was "hajji"—he was an Iraqi man, Iraqi nationality—we, my whole platoon, thought it was funny. Ha, ha, Iraqi man blew himself up laying an IED. So, you know, that's how we dealt with that kind of stuff—we thought it was funny. It was either laugh about it, cry about it, or say nothing and go insane. So we laughed about it. We're big burly men and we're not allowed to cry, so we laughed about it, yeah.

Abusing Dogs for Fun

Other than that, that was all that really ever happened in Bi'aj. They abused dogs. There was one dog in particular that they beat the hell out of: slit its throat, smashed its skull with a shovel, cut its belly open, broke its leg. They thought it was all fun and games. The commander at Bi'aj had a rule that he was allowed to hunt dogs—like shoot dogs on post—he was allowed to do it, but nobody else was. One day he damn near took out one of my platoon members with a ricochet because he missed the dog. The bullet ricocheted off a nearby wall and up into a guard tower, 'bout damn near took off my platoon member's head. But the commander never got in any trouble for that, because it was never reported that a soldier came inches away from death from a ricocheted bullet fired by a company commander.

Even though there was this rule of the commander's, they went ahead and killed the dog. The reason for that was because they didn't like it, because it hung out next to one of our OPs [observation posts], one of our guard towers, guard points. We had a guard point right next to the front gate. The guard point was nothing more than an NCO sitting in the truck listening to the radio, and a specialist or below sitting in the gunner's hatch. The dog that they mutilated, we called it the guard point dog because it was always there, sitting underneath the truck, walking around the truck, begging for food and scraps or whatever. Well, they didn't like that for some reason, so they killed it. What made it worse though was, again, we thought it was funny, including myself: laugh about it, cry about it, or say nothing and go insane. So we laughed about it. About a week later we found out that the dog was female and had had puppies. They caught and killed the puppies and buried them right next to the guard point, making a nice little wooden cross that said "guard point puppies." Ha ha, ho ho, hee hee.

But Bi'aj was safe. We had daily mortars, but they never really came close. They had, what—two—that landed inside our safety zone. One of them hit my tent, but we weren't there when it happened. We were out and about doing our mission, so we came back and our tent was gone. The only people that were on the FOB [forward operating base] at the time were the guards. Everybody else was on mission. So they hit an empty tent and destroyed some personal shit: computers and TVs and whatever. But other than that, it was safe in Bi'aj.

Ramadi—Hell on Earth

While we were in Bi'aj, my platoon was attached to Cav [cavalry] scouts. We're the cavalry scouts' support. They need artillery, we give it to them; they need an extra rifle, we give it to 'em; they need an extra hand in anything, we give it to them: that's our job, to support Infantry and Cav scouts. Well, in Iraq our mission was to support Cav scouts, which we did in Bi'aj for five months.

Well, then, after that, Uncle Sam decides to take our unit and move it from Bi'aj to Ramadi. Ramadi was hell on earth. Ramadi was just hell on earth. We get to Ramadi and our mission changes a little bit, from just doing area patrols and whatever to doing raids. So, we get military intelligence that says, "Hey, this guy is a known terrorist or known bad guy and he has this, this, and this in his house," so we've got to go in and get it. That's what our mission was in Ramadi. That's what our mission was supposed to be. But my battalion commander decided that my platoon was too valuable an asset to lose to such a mission, such a hazardous mission, so he took us back. He took us away from the Cav scouts and sent the Cav scouts in alone to do this mission, and switched our mission to a relatively safer one, basically. And the Cav scouts got mutilated. I'll say it: the Cav scouts, they got their asses kicked in Ramadi.

I can't remember how many memorial services I went to where I talked to the guys afterwards and they told me about what was going on. Their commander was sending them down black routes, which is a road that it's a 100 percent chance that you're going to get hit, whether it be IED or small arms. You don't go down black routes, because it's 100 percent that you're going to get hit. You're going to get hit by something. So they have routes and whatnot mapped out so you know where to go and where not to go. Well, their commander would send them down black routes because it got them to their objective faster. Halfway to the objective, they'd have to turn around and come back because they were loaded down with casualties, dead or otherwise.

I kept hearing about this, and I'm like, "Well, what the hell—we're supposed to be there for these guys' support and they don't have the support they need. They're getting pinned down by small-arms fire, and if we would have been there we could have called in artillery. They would have had an extra rifle firing friendly rounds. I don't know; that's our platoon's job, to support these guys." And we weren't because we were "more valuable" than someone else.

Convoys under Fire

My convoys got hit a few times. Luckily, my truck never got hit, but my convoy, my platoon was hit, and luckily we didn't lose a lot of people from my platoon. We lost one guy—he didn't die but he lost an eye—and that was pretty much it. And we had another incident where we had been on our way out to an OP [observation post] and as we were rolling out the gate, we got stopped and given an order to escort a few paperweight-pencil-pushers, desk-jockeys, office pokes, people who had never been outside the wire for combat situations, no clue what they were doing, but we're supposed to escort them from Camp Ramadi to camp TQ [Al Taqaddum] so they can fly home on leave or some stupid shit like that. I don't know what they were doing, but we had to escort them to TQ.

One of the trucks gets hit. One of the guys that's going home on leave is hit, injured bad. And my platoon did its job. We set up a safety perimeter. We put our trucks where they needed to be, started trying to call up for Med-Evac and found out that our radio frequencies were being jammed by the paper-pushers because they were trying to be heroes and prove that they could do whatever it was that we did. They were trying to call in for Med-Evac as well, but they kept boxing it up. While all this was going on, I was assisting the medic and trying to keep the man alive. Needless to say, the soldier didn't make it because a few NCOs thought that they wanted to try to play hero and G.I. Joe and they wanted to try to call for Med-Evac when they had no clue what they were doing.

He literally died while I was holding his head. I was kneeling on the ground, holding his head, keeping it elevated, doing whatever it was that the medic was asking me to do. I'm pretty positive that the soldier would have died anyways even if the Med-Evac would have gotten there, because he had damage just everywhere, there was shrapnel—I'm not talking about Hollywood chunks of shrapnel the size of the Titanic sticking out of him—there was just shrapnel just embedded everywhere in the side of his body. There was a piece of... I think it was a rock or something, I don't know, piece of metal, rock, or something that punctured the side of his jaw, and when it hit his jaw it ricocheted down and ripped off the side of his throat. I'm holding this guy's head, trying to keep him alive, trying to talk to him, trying to help the medic, and we can't call for Med-Evac, and the soldier died in my arms because somebody else wanted to try to play hero.

Keeping It All Bottled Up

You know that phrase I used earlier: laugh about it, cry about it, or say nothing and go insane? Well, I chose to say nothing. For the longest time, I never even thought about it again. After it happened, I never even glanced at it, never thought about it, never dreamt about it, never talked about it, nothing. It happened, it was over, carry on with your mission. Well, I carried on with my mission, not ever talking about it or whatever. It's just that, you know, bottle it up inside, it builds pressure, and eventually the cork blows? Well that's pretty much what happened.

I think it was like two weeks later or something, we were preparing to go out on another route clearance mission. While we were preparing, explosions and gunfire started going off in the city. Well, that wasn't our job, so we didn't care about it. Whatever. Somebody else's problem. We're going to deal with ours. We're going to continue getting ready for our mission, and we're going to go about our own business. Well, we get stopped at the gate because we can't leave the gate when there's gunfire so close. So we're just sitting there waiting for it to end. After about fifteen minutes the gun battle finally ends.

Because it was right across the street, quite literally right across the street from the front gate, about five minutes after it ended we had a bunch of Iraqi police trucks—these white

Chevrolet pickup trucks that they use for their police vehicles—start pulling in the front gate and the backs of them are loaded with dead—not just wounded but dead—soldiers. And I'm not talking about a few bodies in the back. I'm talking these trucks, five or six trucks, loaded, piled on top of each other, with dead bodies, dead Iraqi police. The last truck that came in only had four bodies in it, but they had let the tailgate down. Sitting on the tailgate, this large, fat, Iraqi police member had been hoisted on the tailgate. And laugh about it, cry about it, or say nothing and go insane; we laughed about it. Who cares? They were Iraqi. "Oh, and by the way, did you see that fat fucker on the last truck?" Because he was, he was a huge guy. Every bump they hit, you could see his fat jiggle. It was ridiculous, because he was only halfway on the truck as it was, and because he was so large, every bump they hit his fat jiggled and shifted his weight—he about damn near fell off the back of the truck. And so, we laughed about it—ha ha, the Iraqis can't fight as well as we can, whatever, and did you see that fat fuck on the back truck? After that, nothing was ever said about it.

To be honest, I had completely forgotten about that, about the trucks. It wasn't until about seven or eight months ago I was sitting here talking to one of the NCOs from my platoon, he and I were sitting here talking about some shit that had happened there. He mentioned it and at first I had no clue what he was talking about, no clue. I thought he was just bullshitting with me and making shit up. Then he explained, "No, man. The truck that came in that was loaded with dead IPs. You don't remember that, man? You were a gunner at that time, you should've seen it." And he kept trying to explain it to me and I couldn't remember. Then he mentioned the fat man on the back truck, and as soon as he mentioned the fat man on the back truck, it came back to me like a dam had just broken open or something, and the first five minutes of remembering it was like I was there again watching these trucks roll in. Then he goes, "Well wasn't it like two weeks before that…" and then he brings up the story where the soldier dies in my arms.

That was a real bad month for us: soldier dies in my arms, two weeks later we get a convoy full of dead IPs, every day for three or four weeks after that we were attending memorial services. I don't know. I got lucky, in the sense that I was never actually in an actual gun battle. I got lucky in that sense. But as far as dead bodies, dead battle buddies, I saw my fair share. There's a lot of other stuff that happened in Iraq that I can't even talk about, just stupid shit like that that just bears on my mind every single day. I got to think about the stupid shit: the dog, the guy that blew himself up, the truck full of people, the battle buddy dying in my arms, the chain of command stupidity. Every day I've got to think about this and try and deal with it. And the Army, their way of trying to help is to give me pills and get me doped up so I forget about it, or so I don't talk about it.

Problems with PTSD

When we got back from Iraq, we went to a reintegration thing for like three weeks or something like that. During that three weeks they sent us to a doctor and the doctor says, "Is there anything you guys want to talk about, whatever?" and 98 percent of the people say, "No. Fuck no. We've been in Iraq for fifteen months, we don't want to be cooped up in a shrink's office rehashing everything that happened. We want to be going out partying, getting drunk, whatever." So that's what we did. It wasn't until about two months later that I started having nightmares, and I started getting really tense and nervous and anxious about everything. A car door slams too hard and I freak out. Driving down the road, even now—this is a year later, a year later—I still, driving down the road, find myself looking on the sides of the road. I'm not just spacing out, I'm *looking* for things: tripwires, pressure plates, shit that's not supposed to be there.

When I walk past people, I find myself being suspicious of them, especially if they have their hands in their pockets. Every time I leave my room, I pat my chest—a year later, a year down the road and I still look for my weapon. I pat down my chest looking for the strap, and if it's not there, then it clicks, and okay, yeah, hello, you're not in Iraq anymore; you don't have a weapon. I used to go back into my room searching for my weapon, and it would take me five or ten minutes to realize that, hello, wise guy, you're in Germany not Iraq. You don't have a weapon.

Trying to Feel Human Again

Two, three months later, I had all these problems, all these issues, and because of the platoon I was in I was scared to go to anybody for help. Because my platoon was, you know, the John Wayne handbook prodigy: tough skin, tough guys, big burly tough guys, don't cry, don't talk about problems, and whatever, and all that macho bullshit. So instead of talking to anybody about it, I started burning myself to feel human, because a lot of shit that happened downrange wasn't human.

I used matches, lighters, cigarettes, whatever. Because I'd done it repeatedly, I would put blister on top of blister on top of blister, so I had a good four or five inches of just blistered skin on the palm of my hand. When that got too unbearable for me I would move to the wrist, or I'd move to the other hand, or I'd move to the joints in the fingers, and then I would let these heal, and the whole time I would squeeze them—instead of burning myself again I would put enough pressure on the blister to make it hurt, and "All right, you're still human, whatever, I guess." Then after they healed, I'd just do it again. So about every month or two, I'm burning myself to keep blisters and pain involved just so I know that I'm real, that I'm human.

They never caught me in the act, but they saw the blisters on the palm of my hands. That's the only place I ever did it—occasionally I'd do it on the wrist or on a finger or something—but on the palm of the hands because it was less likely that it'd be seen and I'd be caught. Well, I got caught anyways, and instead of, "Hey, man, do you need to sit down and talk about something, you maybe want to go to the chaplain or maybe a mental health specialist—do you want to talk about something?" No, no, no, no: "Hey, man, did you know you can get in trouble for damaging government property?"

I was pissed. I was furious. For one, I'm already having problems because I got this feeling like I've turned into a machine—a machine that can kill without second thoughts, a machine that can look at a dead person and laugh about it. So I'm already having a little bit of identity issues, and now I'm told that I'm *government property*, and I'm *damaging* it? All right, well, fuck you very much, Uncle Sam. I'm done. If this is how you're going to react to a soldier having a problem, I'm done. I quit. So I went AWOL. I went AWOL for twenty-nine days and turned myself in.

Pills, Pills, Pills

When I turned myself back in at Giessen, I told my commander about what was happening. So the one month I was in Giessen before it closed, I was seeing a mental health specialist, and she gave me a mental health referral for a discharge, saying that for the betterment of the Army it would be better if I got out.

So I went back to Dexheim and I started seeing a mental health specialist in Wiesbaden. She never really said much. It felt like, when I talked to her, like talking to a brick wall. Every time the only thing she ever said to me was whenever we were about to close session, she would refer me to another doctor: "You know, I can refer you to Dr. so-and-so because he can give you pills—pills for your insomnia, pills for your anger, your aggression, your anxiousness, whatever." Pills for everything, basically. I kept telling her I didn't feel comfortable with pills. She never asked why, so one day I just told her straight up that I wasn't comfortable with pills because after I came back from Iraq I was suicidal. Before I started burning myself I was suicidal. I had attempted suicide hundreds of time by taking countless amounts of pills—Aleve, Tylenol, whatever—and downing them with bottles of vodka. I'm lucky as sin that I'm still alive, the amount of pills and alcohol I downed to try to go out peacefully or whatever… I don't know. But even after I told her why I wasn't comfortable with pills, every other time I saw her, she was still, "Hey, we can give you pills for this and you don't have to worry about the suicide thing because it'll be controlled."

Well, whoop-de-fucking-doo, I don't care if it's controlled. I don't feel comfortable with pills and I don't want your damn pills. What I want is for you to sit down and listen to me. I want you to talk with me and have a conversation with me, give me some advice and some opinions, but I don't want your damn pills. But every time I went in there, she'd fill out for more pills for me. It got to the point where I felt like standing up and just walking out. It started to piss me off real bad, because she just wasn't listening to me. If she wasn't listening to me about the fact that I don't feel comfortable with pills, I don't think she was listening to a damn word I was saying about anything that happened downrange or anything that was troubling me. She was just there to collect a paycheck. So I said, "Screw her."

I kept going to her, hoping that maybe she'd get it through her thick skull, but I also started seeing the chaplain. I'd go talk to the chaplain every now and then—I'm not even religious. But I was looking for somebody to talk to. Then the *chaplain* started doing the same damn thing: "Hey, you know, I can give you a referral to go see Dr. so-and-so and he can get you pills." "Well, that's great, sir, but I don't feel comfortable with pills." Well, then, the same damn thing. I told him why I wasn't comfortable with pills, but every other time I went and saw him, "Hey, you know, I can give you a referral to go see Dr. so-and-so." "That's great, sir, but I don't like the idea of pills."

AWOL One More Time

In October they told me that they weren't going to discharge me—they were throwing my chapter packet out the window, because going AWOL for twenty-nine days wasn't a serious enough offense to be chaptered on a Chapter 14, commission of a serious offense. I was like, "All right, well, what're you guys going to do to me?" "Well, we're going to give you an Article 15, we're going to demote you one rank, and we're going to give you forty-five days extra duty and forty-five days restriction, and then we're going to send you to Fort Campbell." Well, that's great, 'cause Fort Campbell is redeploying in a few months. "Yeah, well, you know, you did sign a contract, so you just have to suck it up and drive on." Which I did. I served my forty-five and forty-five. I wasn't necessarily the best soldier and I wasn't the worst. I was just there, just kind of passing in and out of time, not knowing what I was going to do.

But I *can't* be in the military. It's not that I don't want to be; I can't. I can't stand being around people in uniform, I can't stand being in uniform, because every day all it is is a constant, twenty-four-hour, seven-days-a-week reminder of not only what I did but what I witnessed and kept my mouth shut to.

So in December, late December, just after Christmas, I went AWOL again. This time I was gone for forty-some-odd days. I'd become a deserter. So now I've gone AWOL twice, the second time I became a deserter, and I straight-up thought I was going to Mannheim; I thought I was going to prison. I was ready to go to prison just to prove my point. One, I refuse to be in the military anymore, and two, another point I want to get out is that I don't agree with the Army's treatment for soldiers—their treatment for everything, it doesn't matter what it is, their treatment for everything is pills. It does not matter what the problem is, whether it's physical, mental, or otherwise, pills is the answer for everything, and I don't like that. Now, I agree, in some situations pills are necessary. For maybe an actual, physical sickness, medicine is fine, but when it comes to the mental things, pills are not the answer because all that's going to do is you're going to grow to think that you actually need these pills and it's going to become like an addiction. Well, if I wanted to get addicted to a drug, I'd go buy a gram of coke. I'd go buy a baggie from somebody and smoke a joint. If I wanted to get addicted to something to drown my sorrows, I could do it without the Army's consent.

So I went AWOL from Dexheim, thinking that I was going to prison. I just made it simple and turned myself in at Wiesbaden because there's an MP station in Wiesbaden. So I turned myself in at Wiesbaden, spent that night in a holding cell at the MP station.

Next morning, an NCO walks in, says, "Hey, shave, take a shower, put these PT clothes on. You're going to go see your new commander." And the whole time I'm thinking, well maybe they're just going to try to fuck with me some more, because I turned myself in on the eighth of February and I was supposed to report to Fort Campbell on the tenth. So I figured maybe they were just going to stick me on a plane and send me to Fort Campbell. But no, they took me to a commander here in Wiesbaden, and the commander says, "Well, we ain't sending you to Mannheim, but we're going to give you a Chapter 14"—pattern of misconduct and commission of a serious offense. I said, "All right," and he goes, "And we've talked to your lawyer and we've made a deal with him and this is how things are going to work: we're going to try to get it over as fast as possible." Well, that was at the beginning of this month and, from what I've been told, some time this week my paperwork should go through. Once my paperwork goes through, I'll have another week of out-processing and then I should be done with the Army.

Enough Hell

I've gone through enough hell, and. I'm not trying to be arrogant, or snotty, or whatever, but I feel that I deserve some good times, because I'm only twenty-one and I feel like I'm forty years old. I've done nothing but try to do good things, and every time I … it's like the harder I try to do something good, the harder it crashes down on me. So I think I'm due for some good times coming up.

David Cortelyou was discharged in Germany and lives there now with his wife. A film about the two of them, Das Eine zeiht das Andere so nach *(English title,* Repercussions*) was released in Germany in October 2010.*

Hart Viges

September 2008

Benjamin Hart Viges joined the U.S. Army in 2001 immediately after the events of 9-11. He was eager to fight against those he saw as America's enemies. Hart spent a little less than a year in Iraq and on his return experienced some symptoms of PTSD. Little by little, he began to rethink his support for the war and eventually realized that he was a conscientious objector. He was honorably discharged from the military in 2004 and today is a member of Iraq Veterans Against the War.

I went into the military November 1, 2001. I joined because of September 11. I felt I needed to contribute to a solution and I felt the way I could best do that was join the military. Ever since my youth, I always thought if America was ever invaded or attacked, I would join the military. I was twenty-six. When I joined, I was living in Seattle, Washington, Kirkland to be more exact, and I was managing a restaurant. At the time I played the bass making music with my friends, just bought a new car. I was living a pretty good life. I definitely made a transition in my life when I joined. It was something I felt pride about at that time.

When I walked into the recruiting office on September 12, 2001, I asked for Infantry and Airborne and I ended up with the Eighty-Second Airborne Division, First 325 HAC Battalion mortars. I was a mortarman. I went to Basic Training at Fort Benning and that's where I also had my AIT and jump school. I remember the drill sergeant came up to me and looked me in the face and said, "You are an old man aren't you?" I didn't really know how to respond, just said, "Yes, drill sergeant."

Jump school was pretty easy for me. We'd just had Basic Training, so we all were in pretty good shape and it's what I signed on to do, jump out of airplanes. I actually got pushed out the door my first jump. As I walked down the line, airborne shuffle and all that, I made my turn to the door and thought: "Oh my God, what I have got myself into?" and then, boom! Out I went. You are supposed to say, "One thousand, two thousand, three thousand, four thousand," to count before the main parachute opens up and I thought to myself, "Oh my God I'm gonna die, Oh my God I'm gonna die, Oh my God I'm gonna die," and the chute opened up and I thought, "Oh my God I'm gonna live, Oh my God I'm gonna live." When I landed I looked up in the sky and saw the bird that I jumped out of and I was definitely hooked on jumping out of airplanes. I was very motivated all throughout my training. Even when I got to my unit I was motivated.

In Kuwait, Preparing for Iraq

I was deployed to Kuwait in February 2003. We were there for about a month, training and planning to jump into the Baghdad airport. It was said that we weren't going to jump our trucks, so we would have to jump with our mortar systems. So we trained running around the camp in Kuwait with mortar equipment strapped to our rucksack.

I was lucky enough to have a base plate for a mortar on my rucksack. It was kind of balanced, even weight. But still the weight of our load was probably close to a hundred pounds. I found a way to get up with the heavy rucksack by flipping over onto my chest, doing a push up, and throwing a knee up and kind of doing a squat up. But by doing this, my knee had a reemergence of an old injury that I hadn't told the Army about because I wanted to be Airborne. Back in high school, I had hyperextended my knee and torn some cartilage. Now the same knee there in Kuwait was blowing up to the size of cantaloupe and was getting pretty painful. I was basically hiding that injury because I wanted to jump; I felt that I didn't want to be held back for any reason. But my sergeant saw me walking funny and he asked me what was going on, and I told him I didn't want to be held back. So he just took me to the medics and without any paperwork they gave me some anti-inflammatory pills and just told me to stay off the leg for a while so I was pretty much stuck in my the bunk in the tent.

My knee healed up and our plan changed. The Third ID [Infantry Division] was ahead of schedule and they already took Baghdad so they scratched our jump into Baghdad airport. Then when we heard 173rd out of Vicenza had jumped into northern Iraq, we were all pretty pissed. We wanted a jump to get our mustard stains, so to speak, our little part of gold cluster on our wings to say that we jumped in a combat area. But instead, we unloaded our mortar systems and everything we were to jump with and got our trucks out, and we drove in March 2003 to southern Iraq.

Into the Combat Zone

The first Iraqi I ever saw was a dead man sitting in the passenger seat of a car near the border. It was kind of like an SUV-type truck, painted in what we later found out were taxi colors. People would paint their cars in orange and white to mark them as taxis. A nice "welcome to Iraq" sign.

Seeing that dead man just kind of sharpened my mind more, knowing that I am going into war. We were all psyching ourselves up for it, that whole mentality of really trying to dehumanize people. We actually started back at Bragg when we knew we were being deployed. One of the guys in our platoon found a video of Chechnya's soldiers chopping off the heads of Russians. There were two particular videos that we watched multiple times, one with sound and one without sound, but they were morbid to say the least.

The first town we went to was in the south, called As Samawah. The supply line was getting hit pretty fairly often from there, so we were assigned to go and take the town. We came up to As Samawah and they positioned us in this, oh my God, covered up trash dump. If we dug not too far down we would find trash. This was outside town about a mile or two—you could definitely see the outline of the town. One morning, the line companies marched into the town and when the fighting started, we could hear the fire fights all day long, and we got fire missions to fire mortars into the town. We'd see an attack helicopter shooting missiles, F-18s dropping the biggest bomb I've ever heard go off, the Specter Gunships—C-130s equipped with artillery guns and these super Gatling guns. I really don't know the nomenclatures for those, but they just looked like a streak of white lightning.

After I guess we killed enough people from that shelling, we moved into the town and it's just a bit unreal to just see the amount of destruction in the city. I saw dogs fighting, donkeys fighting, birds fighting in the sky. It really seemed like the violence from humans fighting spread out to the rest of the life that lived there.

We ended up taking this abandoned hospital that seemed to have been turned into a training ground for Fedayeen. We posted up there inside the town, and it was basically pretty quiet. From there we never got attacked. But maybe five hundred meters out, there were these huge storage tanks, and every once in a while you'd see someone go over there and work in the tanks and come out with these buckets. After about a week, the rest of the town caught on and there was a huge line getting whatever from these huge tanks. We found out that they were taking gasoline. The tanks were storing gas.

Since we were the closest unit to the gas tanks, we were ordered to stop the people taking the gas. We rolled out there and these people were coming out with these cans of gasoline and I remember one of my sergeants raised his rifle and in his Texan accent said, "Drop your weapons," in Arabic. I told the sergeant, "Sergeant, you are telling him to drop his weapon. He doesn't have any." He said, "Well, he knows what I mean." Luckily, no one got shot that day.

It just kind of seemed a bit odd to me, to see the poverty of that town, what it went through, to think that they went through thirty years under Saddam. They should at least get free gas. But I didn't really question my orders at that time.

I was questioning that action, but not the war itself. There were Iraqi guys with one ear who would come up to our position and would thank us for being there. When they refused to fight for Saddam, they got an ear taken off. There was a good amount of cheering and waving to us. "Yes Bush! No Saddam!" we would hear from kids and people. I was still feeling like we were doing good.

We were there for a month, then moved to a different position closer in town. We came up to a position where we saw a destroyed Humvee and we knew what had happened with it. It was an armored Scout. It was back when we were out in the dump outside the town. On the radio we heard this call for help, screaming, "We're hit, we're hit." Apparently an armored Scout went too far out of its position and got destroyed. Couple of guys died in that truck. Then we crossed over the bridge where it was attacked from and saw the burnt-out Iraq truck that attacked it. It was probably hit by a missile of some sort after it attacked the Scout. It was a bit scary on that bridge, right there on the Euphrates.

Coping with the Violence and Fear

I was just trying to gather my happy thoughts throughout that whole thing. What I deemed my happy thoughts were that I could touch right there. America basically disappeared in my mind. I broke up with my girlfriend at the time from there in Baghdad. I would get letters every now and then, but I didn't think much of America. All I had were my puppy doggies, my Italian music video, my chocolate banana milk. If I had those things, I was good.

I love dogs, and there are plenty of them there, mostly wild. Iraqis don't really hold much regard for dogs. Shepherds would use them for their herd. But other than that, platoons all over the place were adopting dogs. It was just a really healthy thing for us.

But this other post decided that the dogs were no help for us so they killed them all off. There was talk that they were going to do that to us, but it never got implemented.

Problems Didn't Stay Behind

I learned that things kind of follow you home. The first night we were back, me and a couple of guys we went straight to the strip club right before it closed. Coming back there was a bag of trash on the side of the road and I swerved my car away from it. I pretty much went into the oncoming lanes, but luckily there wasn't any traffic so there was no car wreck. Pretty much everyone in the car was silent. I remember Cosmo saying "Hey! We are back in America, man," and I was like, "I know, I know. You don't need to tell me twice." It was that jerk reaction. I later learned that it was post-traumatic stress… learning these patterns of survival and helplessness, modes that no longer really applied to what was going on here. But at that time I just didn't know what was going on.

A year or two later, I really searched for help but that was really met with resistance at the VA clinic here in Austin. One doctor particularly who said I didn't need any help because I have too much positive stuff in my life. He was talking about the peace movement I was part of at that time.

Change of Heart

The change started in San Angelo, Texas. When I was on leave, I went to see my family, my mother and my stepfather. There was a party, an artist's opening. I met a woman and she was talking to me and arguing with me about what it is to be a soldier in the war. I was arguing with her that we did a good thing; we got rid of Saddam. That was my last strain of justification for what we did over there. We got rid of Saddam; I didn't care for the weapons of mass destruction at the time. I pretty much knew then that we fed them weapons of mass destruction to fight the Iranians. But it really wasn't my job to question. My job was to follow orders, to watch out for my brothers to my left and right. But she made an impact on me. We fell in love. But, yet, I couldn't find the language to explain my feelings.

In those same two weeks, I traveled around the country a bit—saw family in California, saw my friends up in Seattle where I joined up. In Seattle, my friends and I went to see *The Passion of the Christ*. When I came out of the movie theater, I came head on with the question of, how can I be a Christian and live the teachings of Jesus and be a soldier at the same time?

I went back to my unit from that leave period and basically just put on a mask. I wasn't really looking at these questions and experiences that I had. I was still talking with Alejandra, the woman I met in San Angelo. I was basically denying my feelings so much that I was giving myself, I guess, stress attacks. I felt like someone was trying to cut out my chest with a knife. I felt these sharp pains over my heart and my left arm would go numb. I felt light-headed and couldn't breathe. I thought I was having these little heart attacks. So I went to the hospital there on Fort Bragg and got tested: chest x-ray, EKG, blood tests, and I pretty much came clear on all the tests. They narrowed it down to that the protective sac around my heart was being inflamed and they said one of the possibilities for this is stress. They asked me about my stress and I said, "No, no, I'm not stressed." They gave me some anti-inflammatory pills and gave me this "No PT for two weeks" note for me to take back to my platoon sergeant.

When I handed the note to my platoon sergeant, he asked me what was going on and I told him what happened. He asked me am I stressed and that's when I just kind of broke down. I have a lot of respect, still do, for my platoon sergeant, Sergeant Stone. I just burst out crying, saying, "They are going to fuck me, sergeant, they are going fuck me." He was like, "Why, why are they going to fuck you?" I said, "I am not going to pull the trigger. I am not going pull the trigger." He really surprised me. He calmed me down, went up and closed the door to his office, sat me down and said, "War affects people in different ways. Would you like to go talk to the chaplain about this?" I said, "Sure."

Becoming a Conscientious Objector

The very day I went to see the chaplain, Chaplain Chester, I told him everything that I felt. Though I couldn't really put a word on it, he asked me if I was a conscientious objector. I said, "Well, that sounds about right." He said, why don't I think about if for a couple of days. I go and Google it and I find all this information. From there my platoon sergeant, my chaplain, and I believe my first sergeant, went to see the sergeant major to see if I can't be moved from mortar platoon to chaplain's assistant, to see if being in that environment would help me come to terms with my new feelings.

When they moved me to chaplain's assistant, I was able to work even more on my conscientious objection packet. I went to the Fayetteville Peace House and had excellent conversations, got some information, actually got a copy of Jeremy Hinzman's conscientious objection packet. I saw how he was messed with greatly, and he went up to Canada with his family.

As chaplain assistant, I would pretty much do the work that the chaplain gave me before lunch, and the rest of the time I would be up in my room. I just bought a new computer and I was working on my conscientious objection packet.

About month later, when I was done, I turned it in and it was about ten months later in December 2004 that I was honorably discharged as a conscientious objector. I see those months as my finest time in military.

Iraq Veterans Against the War

I am the chaplain of the Iraq Veterans Against the War chapter here in Austin, Texas. IVAW is growing, definitely. We are gaining members all the time, going to conventions and rallies and the scene. They are my extended family and always a blessing.

I am opposed to all wars. When anybody picks up a tool to violently fight their brother or sister, I am opposed to it and do not support it. I finally found my fight, my good fight. It's the path that I am most comfortable with, more comfortable with myself than I have ever been in the rest of my life.

William Shearer

June 2008

William Shearer joined the U.S. Army at the age of seventeen. After Infantry and Airborne training, he was deployed to Iraq. While there, Shearer had some serious personal problems and found that the Army was very unresponsive and unsupportive. He began to develop concerns about the way the Army treats its soldiers. When he returned to the U.S, Shearer was diagnosed with PTSD. He received no meaningful treatment for this and at some point decided he was going to find a way to get out.

I enlisted in 2002, when I was seventeen. I just grew up being taught that that's being patriotic, taking care of my country. That's all I ever wanted to do. I went to Basic Training in Fort Benning, Georgia. I was in the Infantry. After Basic and Infantry training, I went to Airborne school.

I was with the 1st battalion, 509th Airborne Infantry. They weren't actually a deployable unit when the war started. They were pretty much teaching other units what they needed to know before they went over to a combat area. We pretty much put them through a month-long simulation of combat.

Deployment to Iraq

I deployed with that battalion in 2004. There wasn't a lot of action. It's hard to explain. Action over there is like getting IED'd or maybe getting shot at a few times, or a car bomb goes off. It's not exactly what you're expecting when you think of action a lot of times. It's more like hunting season, and you're the deer.

I lost one of my good friends, Sergeant Bret Swank. He was with Alpha Company. An IED went off and ended up killing him. They were dismounted. We lost him and also we lost Anton Brown. Our company was very fortunate, actually. We didn't have any casualties as far as KIA [killed in action] in our company, but the unit we were attached to lost six or seven while we were there.

I watched two of my buddies actually get IED'd. They walked right up on an IED and just disappeared. They didn't die, which was amazing—I think that I found my religion that day—not a scratch on them. But the people who we suspected as the triggermen of the IED were actually innocent. They didn't show any signs of any explosives on their hands or anything like that. But yet they were casualties themselves. We had one guy take a shot through the head and then another guy had his Achilles heel blown off, and just sitting there listening to a guy moan, trying to keep him awake, you know, this stuff… it'll get to you. It'll get to you.

I wasn't injured or anything. It was more of just getting knocked around a lot: IEDs going off, and you just get scuffed up from regular day-to-day running around.

Personal Problems

The Army is fine as long as you do your job the way you're supposed to. But when it comes down to things you care about, if
you have personal problems that make it hard to do your job,
everything that means anything to you goes right out the door.
It means nothing because that's not what your job is. So if something does happen that's important to you while you're over
there, you can't do anything about it, and the Army's not going
to go out of the way to make sure you're taken care of. The more
you lose and the less they do for you, the more you start to see
how jacked up things really are.

I got married in January, and right after that I got word that
we were getting deployed. Actually, I wasn't even in the companies that were deploying. But something had happened in the two
companies that were deploying, so they picked me up as a plug
and put me into First Platoon. I had just gotten married. I had
two weeks to get all the shots and everything—didn't even get
everything I was supposed to get. I missed out on a lot of trainings. The other guys in the platoon had ample amount time to
prepare. I didn't have so much time. I deployed two weeks later.

My wife and I were just into our marriage and we were having little issues already, you know, and while I was gone it just
got worse and worse and worse. She was starting adultery with
an MP on post, and the whole time my platoon sergeant's wife,
who lived across the street from where my wife lived, was giving
my platoon sergeant information about what was going on at my
house. Every day he would tell me something else. He knew about
what was going on but nothing was done. And the Army did nothing. I couldn't do anything myself. As an infantryman there is no
emergency leave unless it's like a death in the family—especially

when you're in a combat zone. Like I said, everything that means something to you is right out the windows. That doesn't mean anything to the military. They don't care.

At the time I was, what, nineteen, twenty years old. I had already made a huge transformation from being a kid into doing what a man should be doing. It was a whole lot that I was piling onto my shoulders. You can only take so much, especially in a situation like that.

There were some NCOs that I could sit and talk to. Pretty much, though, all that they could really tell you is, "Hey, you need to focus on the task at hand." And they're right—it starts to put everybody else's lives at danger. So that's pretty much the support I was getting, besides talking to other soldiers who were going through about the same thing I was going through. It was more like we were comparing what was going on with each of us.

Coming Home

We were there for ten months, I believe. We flew back from Kuwait and arrived back here and we had our little return-home ceremony, and my wife wasn't there. Then, like two days later, we were starting to clean up our weapons and stuff and I got served divorce papers. The liaison to the post came up and served me divorce papers. I didn't even know that was going to happen. But it did.

I also lost some family members as soon as I got home, too. The more things piled up, I just started to deteriorate as a soldier. It made me look worse and worse. It would get harder and harder, and they didn't care. That's what I'm trying to get across: they don't care. If they don't care, and nobody's helping you out, you start to not care. You just look at everything that's bad; you have no positive whatever coming in.

Diagnosed with PTSD

I was checked out for PTSD. When I got home, they put you through all these tests: you talk to a bunch of doctors. I was diagnosed with PTSD, depression, sleep disorders and other things, and pretty much all they did was just start throwing me pills—kind of like to shut me up, you know, put me in an I-don't-care vegetative state, pretty much just to have me there.

They gave me counseling, but it wasn't for what was going on at home, it was for PTSD, and that was just unbelievable. I can't even classify it as counseling. I was talking to some retired colonel, and she's sitting there, and I would tell her some situations that I was in over there. She would be like, "Oh, I understand," and I'm just like, "How can you possibly understand? Granted you were in the military, but I guarantee you were not in any situation like this." It kind of makes you feel like you're whining almost, you know, the way they talk to you. When that starts happening, you're just like, "whatever"—throw that right out the door. You don't even hang with what they have to offer. You're just like, "It's not even worth it."

Thoughts of Discharge

Even though I wasn't getting any support from the Army, I had actually reenlisted for another five years, because like I said in the beginning, this is what I wanted to do. You know, they give you this idea they're going to take care of you, that things are just one big family, you know. So I was thinking to myself, I was just like, "Man, I've gotta have a restart. I've gotta find a way to get myself out of this and start over—start my life over. I have nothing to work with."

But I realized that I wanted to get out. So I started trying to find out what happened to other guys who got out, asking around: "Hey, what happened to this guy for doing this—did he get an Article 15?" I was not so worried about the disciplinary actions but the discharge. That's what I was really worried about. I was asking around, and AWOL was one of the things that got some guys out. But the one thing that came up for me was: fail urinalysis. I just couldn't fathom anybody you deploy with, or anybody who says they care about you so much, like your battalion commanders do, that they would put you out with a bad discharge, after you'd been serving honorably for four years. I wasn't so sure about AWOL, but I knew for a fact that if I failed a urinalysis, I would be able to get out, and I was pretty confident that I wouldn't get anything worse than a general discharge.

Decision to Fail Urinalysis

I went home on leave and I knew that the day after you get back from leave you're going to get a urinalysis test. I thought, "That's how I'm going do it." That was in December of 2005.

A couple weeks went by and then my platoon sergeant called me into the room. I have nothing against my platoon sergeant. He's a good guy and I've known him since Basic Training. He ended up going to my battalion after he got done being a platoon sergeant, so he knew me pretty well. I walked in there and he said, "Shearer, you failed the urinalysis."

Of course they put me in for my Article 15. I did my forty-five days of restriction and forty-five days of extra duty—it wasn't a big surprise to get that. But then I had to go and stand in front of the battalion commander and have him read off my Article 15.

He read it all off and he then he said, "Shearer, you know, you can recover from this." I just looked right at him, and I said, "Sir, I don't want to. I want out."

Up to that point, they were real polite about everything. They treated me like a family member. When I said that, he just did a 180, he was like, "You don't deserve to be in the military." That's when they proceeded to rip off my rank and go about doing the procedures of putting me out. I passed up the court-martial. I got a general discharge under honorable conditions.

Life after Discharge

I haven't even been to the VA yet. I've been nervous to go because I don't want to get pushed under a rug like I feel like I'm going to. I've been to a doctor. He gave me Lexapro for the PTSD and medications for sleeping, but it doesn't help. I mean what can I do? I don't know what to do.

I've pretty much just secluded myself from everything lately. I haven't even had any friends since I got out. When I talk to people, you know, I'll be around family or friends and they'll be talking and I have nothing to say. I feel like an idiot whipping out a war story because that's all I've got, you know? So I just pretty much stick to myself until I get an opportunity to speak with a vet who's gone through what I have.

Reflections on the Military

I feel like they're exploiting those "healthy young bucks" that are just getting out of high school or going to be getting out of high school soon. They're telling these guys all these things they want to hear about how glorious and how fun and how good the military is. But when you do go in, everything changes. One thing I can tell you, you know you could end up in a war zone. What they don't tell you is: you're going to have rules on you that the people you're fighting don't use. They don't abide by any rules. So you're pretty much a pawn. You do what they need you to do regardless how dangerous it is. For instance, you're just driving up and down a road expecting to get blown up. We covered a good strip of highway—it was the most-used transport highway in Iraq. It linked the north and south together, and that's where all the supplies went up and down while we were there. Our job for about two weeks was to patrol that strip of highway and eliminate all threats of IEDs. They don't tell you that you're going to be the person that they pick to walk up to a suspected IED and give it a little nudge to see if it's a bomb, you know. They don't tell you these things, and these aren't things that these kids are thinking about. They don't know this stuff's there. They don't know it's like this.

Kimberly Rivera

December 2007

> *Kimberly Rivera is a wife and the mother of two small children. She is also a GI resister. After enlisting in the Army on two separate occasions and serving three troubling months in Iraq, Kimberly came home on leave and she and her husband, Mario, made the life-changing decision not to return to the war. She and her family drove to Canada, where she is seeking refugee status.*

As most people know, the recruiters start out on you at a very early age in high school, and sometimes they approach you even at sixteen because it's really hard to tell the ages of the kids in high school. Once they find out that you're not sixteen yet, or you're not a junior or senior, they have nothing to do with you. They won't speak to you the rest of the year. But then the next year comes. When they get your rosters from school, they start calling your home; they start setting up their tables again in the lunchroom, and continuing to do their spiel on you over and over and over. As a high school student you're not really prepared, I guess, to make a life-changing decision, and that's what the military is. But I made that decision, and sometimes I feel maybe I was a little forced to do it, being as I lived at home with my mom and dad still, because I was in high school, and I never wanted to be a burden on them. So I thought, well, this would be the best way that I could take care of money for school.

The recruiters had my parents sign some sort of a permission slip or something, to allow them to talk with us. But come to find out that it wasn't a permission slip to allow them just to talk with me; it was a permission slip to allow them to recruit me. But of course, I'm not thinking that the government is playing people like that.

So in 2000 I was a junior and I went in, took the test, and then I next had to talk to a military counselor. The counselor is the one that's actually going to tell me what kind of jobs I qualify for with my scores. They gave me three choices of what I could do. So I chose a job, but not knowing that when I chose my job I was actually signing a military contract. After signing it, I just had to convince myself that I did the right thing, that this was going to be the right choice for me. It happens so fast. As soon as you pick your job you sit in the little room and you basically are waiting to be sworn in. From that moment on, I'm like, "You know what? I just joined the military." I was seventeen.

I went to Basic. Nothing was really real to me. I grew up in Texas. I was always around guns. I was very much a tomboy, so doing that type of stuff, and playing, and doing the little obstacle courses, and do their whole "Kill! Kill! Kill!" stuff was just a game to me, basically. It wasn't real. I'm like, "Hey, what's the best thing I can do: shoot guns, hit guys, and roll with it." I never wanted to tell the drill sergeants that I thought Basic wasn't as hard as volleyball conditioning camp, because I was scared that they would make it harder and then everybody would blame me.

Medical Problems during Basic

During Basic, I started feeling really sick in the morning, just in the mornings, and by afternoon I felt fine. So I went to sick call and on the fourth time, I actually requested a slip for a pregnancy test—which they didn't do, by the way—they did a Pap smear and sat me in a room for the whole day. Then at the end of the day they gave me this little bottle of pills and they said, "Hey, this will take care of all your problems." It was really scary. I get back to my bay and I'm freaking out because I know that the military doesn't want women to have babies. I never did take the pills and just went on with Basic Training. I passed Basic Training in October, and then I went to AIT. My mom slipped me a pregnancy test.

I was about a month into AIT when I actually got the nerve up to do the test. Sure enough, it showed I was positive. So my husband Mario and I were going to have a family and I realized I needed more benefits than just the college money the Army had promised. So I asked what they could do for me. They told me there wasn't much, and we agreed that getting out would be the best thing. Since I was still in training, it was pretty easy to get out.

Economic Hard Times in Civilian Life

I was working at Wal-Mart, and I got to that point in my life that my job was no longer secure. They worked me full-time but only as a "part-time associate," so I couldn't get any of the benefits. It was like walking on eggshells. You're making $10.50 an hour and you're afraid that you're going to be the next person that they're going to fire, because it's easier to pull in somebody else at $7.50 an hour doing your same job.

So I thought, I know a little bit about the Army, why not go back in? I had the honorable discharge. So I signed up again. Everything that a person needs to live successfully with a family, they have in the military. I signed up in the Regular Army as a full-time soldier because I wanted to make sure I had all of the benefits that I needed.

A Military Truck Driver

This time the job I chose was driving a truck, not knowing that that's probably one of the fastest killed-off soldiers that there is in the military. No wonder I got an $8,000 sign-on bonus. The training was only a month long, which meant I wouldn't be so far away from my children for so long.

When I got to my regular unit, the first sergeant said, "Hey, we're getting ready. We're training for Iraq." I felt like I was doing my part in the world, protecting my family and keeping things safe, and I was very anxious to get that combat patch.

One day on CNN I see "30,000 troops will be deployed in October," and I knew I was going to be one of them.

Stressful Times and Troubling Incidents

When I was in Iraq, I wasn't eating, and there were times that I went about a month, a month and a half, without sleeping. Maybe with a couple hours of sleep I would get up and do my eighteen-hour shift and stay up—cleaning my weapon, washing my clothes, just doing the simple tasks of daily life—and then have to wake back up and go right back to duty. It was just really stressful.

I've always felt that soldiers were good guys and the ones that help people when they are in need. They're the ones that rebuild the things and rebuild places. That's kind of how I felt with Iraq. I mean I always thought the purpose there was to gain the hearts of the people, and that was not the case. There were a couple main incidents that happened that made me really question everything, from myself all the way to my service, to why I was there and everything. One of those was when I worked at the front gate. Every single Saturday, civilians came in and put in a claim for restitution. I didn't know what their families had gone through. I didn't know what they had lost. Some of them got the only rifle in the house taken from them, which may have been the only security for their family. Some of them got their young teenage boys and their husbands taken from them and were wondering where they were, and some of them had been traumatically injured.

Well, this one Saturday I remember just clear as day, just like I see everybody now that I approach on a daily basis, like I have never left Iraq. I see this little girl—she was about two years old, maybe, same age as my little girl back home—and I could just see her shaking. It was a violent shake, not a seizure-type shake, but noticeable. Tears were just rolling out of her eyes, rolling down her face. She wasn't weeping. She wasn't crying. Nothing. And kids don't just cry without screaming. I knew something traumatizing happened to that little girl, that she would have tears of trauma rolling down her face. I was helpless; there was nothing I could do. I was in all my battle gear; I was carrying an M16 assault rifle and it was loaded because I was required to keep it on red-safe when I was on the job. I couldn't comprehend how this girl's dad could deal with that, and I couldn't comprehend, being a mom myself, how I would react to my little girl being that way and knowing that I was helpless to do anything to help her or even know what was going on in her mind and what she'd been through. That was very traumatizing for me because I personally couldn't imagine ever seeing my little girl in that situation.

Also at the gates there were older women who were so mature and so proud of being alive. They don't speak a lick of English and they would just come and sit and stare at you while they were waiting to do their claims. In their eyes, piercing your heart and your soul, basically saying, "Why are you doing this to me? What did I do to you? What caused you to want to hurt my family like that?" And you can feel it. They didn't have to say it; you can feel it and you can see it in their faces. I couldn't take that. I can still see people—Iraqi civilians that worked with us—lose somebody that they knew, and they would rip their clothes and fall down on the ground. I had no idea what the heck was going on. That seemed totally unlike any type of grief that I'd ever seen in my entire life. But it was compassion—compassion I'd never seen, never felt, and don't even comprehend to this day. That was amazing to me, that I could see that people that don't even know each other but know what's going on in their lives, that they would have that much compassion for one another that they would be grieving.

A Two-Week Leave

My sergeants knew I was going through a lot of stress, and when I finally got my two-week leave I guess they were afraid that I was not going to come back. So they decided to pull me in and have a little chat about why not to desert. They said basically they could do anything they wanted to me—not just ruin my life, but they could also, if they wanted, make an example of me and kill me during a time of war. That came from their mouths. But by this time there was nothing that they could say or do to scare me straight.

While I was in Iraq, I didn't spare my husband any details about the emotional things that would be going on with me. I was so afraid that I was going to change and not be the person I was when I left. That is just very much the case. I may have those times in my life where my emotions are just running rampant in my soul, and I have these moments of real anger and I just don't understand why, and it was pretty hard for me to handle myself. The only way I can describe it is sometimes feeling like I'm on this roller coaster that goes out-of-control and gets off its tracks and crashes.

So when I got home I was such a wreck and I told my husband all of this. I was so thankful that he was able to step up and find information for me and try and see what it is that he could do to help me.

Contemplating Canada

We were on the Internet one day, and up popped the War Resisters Support Campaign and several stories of different GI resisters. My husband explained to me that we could go to Canada, but I kind of disregarded it: "No, there's not really a way that I could do that—leaving my country." You know, that's a pretty harsh thing to do. That's like rejecting everything you grew up with, everything you've learned, everything you've known of yourself. It's like taking a piece of your identity and flushing it down the toilet, and that's how it felt. But I would rather lose some of the pride, and I would rather lose some of the ideology of America, than participate in fighting and doing some of the things that weren't about protecting my family at home.

On the Road

We couldn't decide what to do so, we figured we'd go on the road, just drive, because I didn't know exactly if I wanted to leave our country or not, everything I knew and everything that we've accomplished being there. It was really hard, really hard. So we just went on the road. We were going to go the long way to Colorado, where I was supposed to report back for duty. We decided that we'd make St. Louis our deciding point, whether we'd go east or we'd go west. But we didn't stop in St. Louis. We drove all the way through Kansas. We spent about ten days just talking with each other, trying to see if this was the right way, what we needed to be doing. Finally we both agreed that what we would be losing wasn't quite as much as we'd thought, and it wouldn't be as hard as long as we were together and had our babies and were happy. So we drove back through Kansas and we started going east. The further and further east we got, the less dread we felt.

We were on the road for about two weeks, in and out of different places. I was super paranoid. I don't know if Mario was, but I definitely was. I've seen the drag-outs myself. In Kuwait, we did the trainings for taking prisoners and clearing out rooms and houses, so I had some sense of knowing exactly what they did on their raids, even though I've never been out on the raids myself. So it's pretty scary having that SWAT-type training and knowing the way that they would take you out.

So we were hopping around a lot. We weren't staying in one particular place, we didn't use the Internet; we didn't get on-line; we didn't use cell-phones even. We took out the batteries, and we took out the SIM cards. That's how strong you felt when you thought you were being pursued.

Crossing into Canada

So we drove up right through Buffalo and we crossed through Canada with our IDs. Of course Mario's not military, and I'm a female so you just don't automatically assume that there is a female soldier wanting to evade the military.

We get through perfectly fine. It was the darkest day you've ever seen. It was snowing and raining at the same time. As soon as we got on the bridge, the birds came out, the prettiest blue sky ever, and a rainbow even. I'm thinking, "It's going to be the right thing here." It was like the best omen. If I had doubts about coming here, I definitely didn't by the time we crossed the bridge.

So we got to Canada and we felt very relieved that we were there, and maybe like I could start my healing process from Iraq and just continue with our lives.

The Canadian government has not made a final decision on Kimberly Rivera's application for refugee status. She still resides in Canada with her husband and family.

Part II:
Rejecting Military Culture

Some active-duty GIs refuse military service because of experiences they have on base, whether it is hearing the horror stories of soldiers returning from war or going through the dehumanizing process of Basic Training. Confronted with the realities of what it means to be in the military and face deployment to a war zone, these soldiers realize that they cannot follow through on their service. This section includes the stories of those who resist war before ever seeing combat.

Military recruiters paint illusory pictures of what young recruits can expect in the military. Teenagers are told a range of lies and half-truths: that if they join, they can likely avoid deployment to a war zone, that the wars are practically over, that troops can quit whenever they want to, that they will become rich off savings from their military salary. A 2007 study by ABC News caught recruiters in the act of lying to undercover teenage recruits, a policy that seems likely to have gotten worse as the U.S. fights two wars and becomes increasingly desperate for boots on the ground.

Recruits are also assaulted with countless ad campaigns touting the adventure of military service and the courage of those who join: in 2008, the Department of Defense spent $7.7 billion on military recruiting and advertising. These ad campaigns make their way into theaters, schools, malls, and even family living rooms, bombarding youth with images and slogans: "The few, the proud, the Marines"; "Army Strong." The military has even been manufacturing video games like *America's Army*, where children can decimate virtual Middle Eastern cities at the flick of a finger.

Once these recruits find themselves in the hands of the U.S. military, reality marks a sharp departure from this fantasy of military life. While each military branch is different, one thing holds true for all: the military must transform young recruits into people who obey authority and who are willing and able to kill when that authority tells them to do so. They must attempt to strip away individual conscience and create an environment where those within the service grow comfortable with, and even enthusiastic about, killing. At the same time, the military strips away identity and conscience and attempts to use basic human impulses of love, compassion, and loyalty toward militaristic ends. Troops are told that they are defending their homeland, families, and freedom, and that the camaraderie they experience with their brothers and sisters in arms is the highest form of community. Thus, service members' good intentions and yearning for collective action are misdirected. The interviews in this section shed some light on what that process looks like as well as what goes on within the military to resist it.

On top of these realities, bases are also filled with troops returning from war. Many who are in training learn about the realities of combat through discussions with those who have been deeply traumatized by their experience. Returning soldiers tell of murdering innocents, living in constant fear, and losing comrades. Slowly, but surely, the fantasy of military life begins to erode.

There are many who find themselves in the clutches of the military and then realize that it is not something in which that they can take part. Here are the stories of those who refused to fight because of what they encountered in a military environment.

Ryan Johnson

November 2007

In January of 2005, Ryan Johnson was a twenty-one-year-old private in the U.S. Army stationed at Fort Irwin in Southern California when he made the decision to go AWOL rather than deploy to Iraq. On January 15, at three in the morning, Ryan and his wife, Jennifer, drove away from Fort Irwin back to their family in California's San Joaquin Valley. From there, they moved to Canada and connected with other resisters in that country.

I grew up in Visalia, California, which is mostly an agricultural district in the San Joaquin Valley. I never really made a whole lot in the work that I did in that area. So one day in November of 2003, me and my wife were looking for a new job and I saw an Army advertisement and thought I'd go down there and check it out. I went to the Army recruiter and they told me about the good pay that I would get, all the benefits, the medical, dental coverage for me and my family, how I would be able to go to college and the bonuses you get when you sign up. It sounded like a good deal. I would get job experience, I would learn a new skill, and it would be something that would help me when I became a civilian again in the future. So I decided to enlist.

Seeking a Noncombat Job

When I decided to enlist, I wasn't interested in becoming a direct combatant. I wanted to serve my country, but I didn't want to be taking people's lives in the process. So when I joined, I requested a job that would be mostly clerical and I ended up getting supply clerk. They told me I'd be in a warehouse in the United States ordering parts, shipping parts because they had soldiers in Iraq and to get supplies to the soldiers in Iraq they need people in the states. That's how they explained it to me.

When I got into the military, I found out that basically even though I was Supply, I'd be sent to Iraq because not only do they need Supply back home, they need Supply there. I also found out that just because I'm Supply that does not mean that they're not going to put me on the front lines. I would have been manning a .50-caliber machine gun on the back of a Humvee.

Ordered to Deploy

When I found out I was going to be deployed, I was shocked, to say the least. But I was a soldier, so at first I just sucked it up. I was just ready to go to Iraq, I packed my bags, and I was going and that was it.

My wife was pretty upset about the whole thing, She was under the understanding that when I signed up I wasn't going to be going anywhere except to maybe Germany.

When we got to our unit, they took friends of mine out of their jobs and put them in completely different jobs—they turned them into truck drivers and they turned them into infantrymen. One of the soldiers I was supposed to deploy with, they took him out of Supply and they made him into a truck driver.

They told the supply clerk to give him a license to drive every vehicle they had in the motor pool. So he was licensed to drive fuel tankers, he was licensed to drive Humvees, deuce-and-a-halfs [two-and-a-half ton trucks], five tons, everything that we had that was a nontracked vehicle. They sent him to Iraq without ever training him on a vehicle. The first time he drove a vehicle was a two-and-a-half-ton truck with twenty soldiers in the back of it on the way from Kuwait to Baghdad.

I didn't get my rifle until a week before I was supposed to deploy, and it was a rifle I hadn't fired before. You know, in Basic Training they have old rifles that are rickety and they gave me this newer rifle that had this folding stock and a scope. I couldn't even fire it. I did not know how to use it properly.

A Fractured Back and War Stories

In November of 2004, when I was at Fort Irwin, I found out that when I had fallen about five months before I had fractured my back. The military refused treatment when I fell, so it took me five months to find out that my back was fractured. After I found that out, they still said they were sending me to Iraq. That's when I started talking to vets that had returned to find out what their experiences in the military were, to find out what their experiences in Iraq were, so I knew what I was getting into, because I'd already jumped into something without getting proper information before when I joined the military.

They were telling me stories of watching tanks running over civilian vehicles in the street. They were telling me stories of abusing civilians, shooting civilians, seeing dead children in the street, firing on vehicles at checkpoints and then when they look inside they find the dead bodies of a family with no weapons, or an incinerated child. Horrible stories that gave them constant nightmares and made it intolerable for them to even be in a public crowded place. They were telling me about when they came home from Iraq their families would take them to Disney World and they couldn't even enjoy it with their family. They had to sit in the hotel room while their family went to Disney World without them.

And I started really looking at how the war began in the first place. You know, looking back at 9/11 and how there was no connection to Iraq. How the president said there were weapons of mass destruction in Iraq but there were none. There was nothing that Iraq was doing to provoke an attack on Iraqi soil. So I began to go even further than just believing that what we were doing was wrong and believing that the entire occupation of Iraq was an illegal and aggressive war.

The Decision Not to Go

The point where I really decided that I wasn't going was literally days before I was supposed to deploy. That's when I called the GI Rights Hotline.

They basically told me that they cannot advise me to go AWOL. Really all they can do is give me the information as to what punishment I could get. They also told me what would happen if I did go to Iraq. They talked to me about the post-traumatic stress disorder. They talked to me about all the horrible things they had heard from other Iraq vets who had come back and called the GI Rights Hotline. There were no specific cases talked about but they did give me an overview of what actually was happening there so that I could make an informed decision.

Going AWOL, Returning Home

When we left, we went back to my family's home. I didn't let my family know what I was doing for their own protection. They knew I'd fractured my back so I told them I was there because of that—they weren't deploying me to Iraq yet because they wanted to make sure my back was ok. That's what I was telling my family. I didn't want them to get in trouble because of me going AWOL because if they'd let me stay there knowingly while I was AWOL, they could be put in prison for it and be charged with aiding desertion, and I didn't want to put that on them.

Two weeks after I left, the Army sent a letter to my mother's house asking me to come back, saying they were worried about my medical condition, and I crumpled it up and threw it away. Two weeks after that, I got another one.

After Five Months at Home, a Move to Canada

The decision to go to Canada was because I felt that I should not have to go to jail or even get a dishonorable discharge because I don't want to participate in something that I find to be illegal. Every soldier has the international obligation to refuse what they see as an illegal order from whichever officer gives it, and I was ordered to go to Iraq by the president of the United States. I have the obligation to refuse that order because I find it to be illegal, and my doing that is upholding international law. So I should not be put in prison for refusing to fight and I don't believe that anybody should.

Before my wife Jennifer and I came up to Canada, we went to Pablo Paredes's court-martial in San Diego and met Camilo Mejía and Aidan Delgado and Pablo. We also met Cindy

Sheehan and many other people that are very important in the antiwar movement. We went home from San Diego. I picked up our gear and drove from Visalia to New York and then from New York to Toronto. When I got there, there were about eight other resisters there. The War Resisters Support Committee was there, too.

They got us places to live. They made sure that we had money to eat and get around. They made sure that we did our paperwork and they helped us to do everything that we needed to do in Canada to get started, basically. After a short time in Canada, you're able to get a work permit; you're able to have a regular job, and get an apartment and just live a normal life—as best you can anyway.

I've applied for refugee status. I went to my original refugee hearing in December of 2005 and was denied, and made an application to appeal, which has been accepted. So I am going to go through the appeals process. But my lawyer adjourned it until after Brandon Hughey's Supreme Court case is heard because right now our cases are based on Brandon's and Jeremy's.

In our original refugee case, the Refugee Board of Canada said that the legality of the Iraq war is not pertinent to our cases. So basically that threw a whole bunch of our evidence out the window. When we were denied, we appealed the decision that the Iraq war is not pertinent, basically putting the legality of the war on trial. We're saying that the war is illegal and it is pertinent to our cases, so Canada will have to allow us to enter that evidence into our cases. We'll have a much better chance of winning at the Refugee Board if we're allowed to make our case that the war is illegal.

No Regrets

Whatever happens, I have no regrets. I don't regret joining the military. I don't regret coming to Canada, because if I hadn't made all those decisions I would just be living in the United States trying to scrape by and I wouldn't know what I know now about what's happening in the world. I was completely ignorant before. I feel that I'm a much better person from what I've done. I was a supporter of the war before. You know, we were supporters of Bush. But everything that I've seen since I joined the military, since I went AWOL, since I've come to Canada, since I've become a political activist, has completely changed my views not only about the United States but everything in the world.

The Canadian government has yet to make a final decision on Ryan Johnson's case. He and his wife still reside in Canada.

Brad McCall

November 2007

> *Brad McCall joined the United States Army in August*
> *of 2006. He had a difficult time making it through Basic*
> *Training but felt a real sense of accomplishment when he*
> *did. At his duty station in Fort Collins, Colorado, McCall*
> *heard stories from vets returning from Iraq that made him*
> *literally sick to his stomach. He began to rethink his position*
> *on the Iraq war and explored the possibility of becoming*
> *a conscientious objector. When that way seemed closed*
> *to him, he decided to go AWOL. A little over a year after*
> *joining up, he left Fort Carson, Colorado, and made his way*
> *to Canada, joining many GI resisters there.*

My boot camp experience went really roughly. I was in Basic
Training a lot longer than a lot of people have to go through
it. When I finally got out, I felt like I had finally accomplished
something for the first time in my life, and I felt like I had really
reached a peak of great achievement for the first time. When
I arrived at Fort Carson, Colorado, my first duty station, all
that feeling of achievement just went to disappointment when
I heard the stories that were being told about Iraq, stories and
details of atrocities that were being committed against innocent people in Iraq. The vets who were telling these stories were

proud of them. They were bragging. They were totally bragging about what they'd done and about what other members of the unit had done. They were laughing about it, and it was just a big joke and they couldn't wait to go back because they enjoyed killing people.

When I heard these, the first thing I did was I ran to the bathroom and, you know, I got sick to my stomach. I could not control myself. It just made me sick. When I got done with that, I went straight to my commander and reported it to him. He said, "Oh, well, we'll have to have a talk with the veterans and make sure they don't tell you guys these stories anymore." That was all that was ever done about it. So from there I really started thinking for myself for once—politically and morally and spiritually—even what my really true hardcore beliefs are. I kind of just rebelled against everything that my parents had taught me as a child and started to try to figure out what I really thought for myself. Kind of got away from that following on the coattails of my parents my entire life.

I found that I wasn't a conservative like I thought I was. I found that the war in Iraq was evil and atrocious and ridiculous, and I found that if I went to Iraq then I would be guilty of war crimes—not to anyone else's mind necessarily, but in my mind. For me, that was enough to draw the line and say, "No, I can't go." If I knew that, when I came back, I would have to live the rest of my life—if I made it back—I'd have to live the rest of my life knowing that I had participated in an evil war for unjust reasons. I would not be able to live with myself. So I took the only step I knew how and applied for conscientious objector status, was laughed at by my chain of command for three weeks while I begged and begged and begged, and finally I left and went to Canada.

Making the Decision

I made the final decision in one day. I talked to a friend of mine in Colorado Springs. He told me about these GIs that are running to Canada, and I was like, "Wow, that's cool." So from there, I went to a friend's house, got on my laptop, and we both saw that it's very possible. We found the resisters website on the Internet, and that night I made the choice that a week later we, which was as a matter of fact payday, we would leave. I knew I would need some cash to get on the road and get moving.

Arrested at the Border

The first thing that happened to me when I got to British Columbia was that I was arrested at the border. The week that I was still in Fort Carson I had e-mail contact with people in Canada that were willing to help me. I didn't realize it, but my parents actually had my e-mail password and they were watching all this go down, and they were forwarding all these e-mails to my commander and first sergeant. So they knew I was going to Canada.

I was arrested at the border by Canadian Border Services on command of the U.S. Army. They put me into a Canadian jail for two days until my lawyer showed up and got me out. He's a young lawyer, Shepherd Moss. He supports the cause. He's an immigration lawyer, and the first thing he told me, he said, "Me helping you guys out is a no-brainer." He said, "I'm not associated with the War Resisters Support Campaign or the War Resisters League or any antiwar group. I'm a lawyer by myself and I'm helping you guys out." And he's a really awesome guy.

While I was in jail I filed a refugee claim, stating that I was requesting to be a refugee from the United States on the grounds that if I return to the United States I will be persecuted or legally prosecuted for my political, moral, and spiritual beliefs.

Seeking Refugee Status

And so that's what I've done. I've started my refugee claim, working on that. Right now it's just a claim. It has to come under review by the Refugee Board of Canada and they will determine whether or not I qualify for refugee status. So far there's only two that have come up to the Refugee Board, only two claims by war resisters, and they have both been denied. They are in the appeals process right now.

My living situation is excellent. I had a couple step up when they heard about me coming in. They stepped up and they took me into their house and they've told me, "You're welcome here," and they've basically said, "We don't want you to leave." These people really, really do help me out. I mean, they give me a weekly allowance, they've given me a cell phone, they feed me every night, you know, it's great.

Unify the Antiwar Movement

I want people to realize that this is a new era of war, and if we don't stop Iraq, Iraq is not going to be the last step that the United States tries to take. It's just the beginning of a long series of wars that I can see in the future. It's not going to be pretty, and we've got to do something about it now. Another thing I would like to say is, we need to unify, to create a united front to fight this. There's no way that all these antiwar coalitions and propeace coalitions can succeed in their goal without being unified. That's how our common enemy is, and that's how we're going to have to be. That's the one thing that's been on my mind here recently, is just unity. That's what I would like everyone to take from me.

Courage to Resist has not heard from Brad McCall since his application for refugee status was denied.

In March of 2005, while stationed at Fort Knox, Kentucky, PFC Robin Long received orders to deploy to Iraq. His opposition to the war in that country led him instead to leave the U.S. and seek asylum in Canada. Nearly deported, Robin was able to postpone deportation at the last minute in order to undergo a Pre-Removal Risk Assessment by Canadian authorities.

I joined up with the delayed-entry program in June of 2003. Basically, I came from a pretty military family—my dad is in the military, aunts and uncles, all of my cousins on my dad's side are in the military. As one of those kids raised on G.I. Joes, I always thought I would be in the Army growing up. When the United States first attacked Iraq, I was told by my president that it was because of direct ties to al-Qaeda and weapons of mass destruction, and at the time I believed what was being said. I was in the Job Corps at the time and I made the decision to join. I felt great about it. I felt like I was finally doing something with my life. I was serving my country. I was going to do something to help.

Dehumanizing Training

In Basic Training, they're trying to break everyone down and build them up the way that the Army wants them to be. We were marching around, singing cadences everywhere about killing people, and blood and guts and gore. They were making us killing machines, and they were kind of dehumanizing the Iraqi people. I was hearing on mainstream media, you know, the United States was going to Iraq for weapons of mass destruction, to liberate the Iraqi people, yet I'm being taught that I'm going to the desert to—excuse the racial slur—to kill rag heads. That at first didn't sit very well with me, so I started asking questions to my drill sergeant, like, "Why are we calling the Iraqi people rag heads?" and he'd say, "Well, that's what they are." And I told them that I really didn't feel comfortable with calling them that. So I was picked on quite a bit. I was kind of the oddball at first, I guess. In the Army you just want to fit in. You don't want to stand out in any way because they'll do things like smoke the entire platoon—"smoke" means like intense physical activity for an extended period of time—while I'm watching them, to make them angry at me, because I don't agree with what the president is saying or what my superiors are saying.

So then, back in the barracks, I get the cold shoulders and don't really have friends, and that got me to shut up for a while. The last month of Basic Training I wasn't voicing my concerns. I'm sure there were people that agreed with me. I never talked to any, because I think they saw the way I was treated and they didn't want that for themselves. So no one would admit to me, but I knew there were some people that were thinking on their own, too.

Stories from Iraq Veterans

Later on, when it came time for our first duty station—I was a tanker—everyone else was getting Fort Carson, Fort Hood, places like that. They stationed me at a nondeployable base in Ft. Knox, which was pretty good for me because it was one way of keeping me from going to Iraq. They were actually helping me out at that time. I didn't have to look forward to going to Iraq any time in the near future.

I guess I'd been at Fort Knox for about four or five months when there were duty-station changes. So there were people from other units coming back from Iraq and stationed at Fort Knox. A lot of them were, I guess, bragging about what was going on over there. We started hearing what wasn't being said in the mainstream media. For instance, one guy had pictures of somebody he ran over with his tank, and another guy had pictures of his first kill—holding a guy's head up and smiling, with a peace sign—and guys bragging about how they'd killed this person or that person, or how they saw this person get blown up. So it kind of started to, I don't know, it started to anger me more than anything. I know I had a really sick feeling in my stomach a lot of the time when I would hear this going on.

Orders to Deploy to Iraq

I thought at that time I really didn't have anything to fear. I didn't feel like I would be going to Iraq. But as the months went on and I started speaking about my concerns about the war again, I got orders to go to Iraq from Fort Knox—from my nondeployable post. The only one in my unit. I got high-priority short-notice orders to meet the occupational requirements of Twenty-Second

Infantry in Iraq, and it basically gave me a month to check out of my unit in Fort Knox and report to Fort Carson, Colorado, and then two weeks later to report to Iraq, on my twenty-first birthday. I hadn't even fired a weapon in probably nine months at that point, because my job at Fort Knox didn't require it.

I was like, why am I the only one getting these? Usually you spend three months at a duty station, but I guess the Army was starting to get desperate for people. I don't know if it was my superiors who volunteered me to go, or what it was, but I was singled out from amongst all those people.

I realized then, "Well, I'm not safe here at Fort Knox anymore. I'm going to have to go and maybe participate in this atrocity and massive killing of the Arab people." But then I was thinking, "Well, if I don't go, then my family's going to disown me, I'll probably get a dishonorable discharge, and have a hard time even getting a job at McDonald's." So I still was kind of up in the air as to what I should do. While I was at home on leave I talked to some friends of mine that are very spiritual people—a couple of them are Buddhists—and they showed me some more accounts about what's going on over there and the behind-the-scenes of the war, and they convinced me that I really couldn't go.

I convinced myself, too. I knew that my conscience wouldn't allow me to go over there. So actually, the day that I was supposed to fly on the plane, I made the final decision that I couldn't go to Fort Carson to check in to go to Iraq. I ended up hiding in a friend's basement for about two months before I met some people that were coming up to Canada—a couple of hippies that were coming up to Canada for a wedding—and I said, "Do you know what? I'm tired of hiding here in the States. I can't work anyways. I might as well go to Canada where at least I won't have to be running from the police all the time." And I went ahead and came up to Canada with them.

Refuge in Canada

I asked the people I was traveling with if we could cross the least-used border crossing in the near-vicinity to where we were going. We were going to Saskatchewan, which is above North Dakota. On the American side they had the big building, three or four cars out in front of it, and the Canadian side was just this little shack with one little old lady in there with a fax machine and a computer, and the only ID I had was my military ID. She actually asked me if I was AWOL, which I later found out they're not even allowed to do, but I told her, "No, I'm just on leave. I'm going to a wedding with these guys." And she's like, "Oh, okay." She just waved us on through, so it was pretty easy for me to cross the border.

I had no idea if there were any other GIs up here. I didn't really look, because I hadn't heard about groups like the War Resisters Support Campaign or anything. I was just coming up to Canada to get away from everything in the States. From Saskatchewan I hitchhiked west and ended up in Nelson, British Columbia, and I met some other traveling people. They were doing a dumpster-diving documentary across Canada, showing how much waste there was, and I joined up with them and hitchhiked from there out to Cape Spear, Newfoundland—St. Johns, Newfoundland—and back again. I met a woman up here named Rene and later had a child with her. When I was staying with her in northern Ontario, I was looking on the Internet and I found the War Resisters Support Campaign. I met with them in Toronto and I was able to meet some other war resisters, and then I didn't feel quite so alone up here. WRSC has given me a lot of direction in claiming refugee status, because before I was just up here on a visitor's visa. I didn't know that I could claim refugee status.

So I claimed refugee status; I got a work permit; I was able to work. I worked for some farms with a national volunteer organization. After that, I was traveling out from Ontario to Nelson to pick fruit, just doing some seasonal work to do some harvesting.

After I had already left Ontario, Immigration sent me a letter that I never got because I hadn't registered my change of address the way you're supposed to anytime you leave. I didn't really have any fixed address at the time. I was just camping in a tent at different orchards, picking fruit to make some money. So they sent me a letter that I didn't receive and didn't respond to, and a warrant was issued for my arrest. I was arrested there in Nelson for that warrant, and just about deported.

I spent a couple of nights in jail in Nelson and was flown from there to Vancouver. I was staying in a holding cell at the airport and the next day I had a hearing to determine whether or not I should be deported. They were trying to get me to sign this piece of paper that was saying that I'm going to waive my rights and allow myself to be deported back to the United States. But I still had the right to claim what is called a PRRA, it's a Pre-Removal Risk Assessment. It's basically like a last-ditch effort. It's kind of like a refugee claim, except refugee claims maybe have a 20–25 percent success rate, and a PRRA has a 2 percent success rate. It's about what risks I would have to face if I went back to the U.S., and that's what's going through right now. It usually takes about two to three months for that to happen. Usually it'll come back and be denied and then you're deported. They say you have thirty days to leave the country once there's been a negative decision on that.

I really don't know what the future holds, so it's really unsettling. I don't know if I'm going to stay here. I don't know if I should make new friends or sink roots down anywhere, because everything could just be taken away. If I do get deported, I won't be allowed—on top of going to jail in the United States—I won't be able to come to Canada for ten years. I have a son up here that I wouldn't even be able to see, so, it's kind of hard to think about that.

If I do get deported, I'm pretty sure they'll be waiting at the border for me. The border patrol probably has a list of all the people that are war resisters up here in Canada, especially people that have been really vocal about things. If I'm deported, then they're definitely going to be waiting there.

Disowned by Most of My Family

My mom is a really—she's a Republican all the way—voted for Bush both times. She doesn't agree with my decision, but she says that people can make their own decisions in life and she doesn't judge me on that. She says that she thinks I made the wrong decision, but she doesn't hate me for it and she hasn't disowned me. But people in my family don't talk to me. My grandparents don't talk to me—on both sides—cousins, aunts, uncles. I've kind of been disowned by most of my family. So I'd rather stay up here in Canada. I've got a lot more people that care about me up here.

I have no second thoughts at all about leaving the Army and coming up here. This is totally better than having to go to that war-torn country and participating in the indiscriminate killing of the Arab people. It saddens me how so many people have been snowballed by it. They just . . . they don't realize that these people have brothers, they have sisters, they have kids, they have mothers, they have fathers just like us. I wouldn't have it any other way. I made the best decision. I know that. Regardless of what hardships I go through, I could've easily caused a family or someone else in that country way, way more hardship. So I have no regrets.

Robin Long was deported by the Canadian government in the summer of 2008. He was handed over to military authorities at the border and taken to Fort Carson, Colorado, where he was court-martialed and given a fifteen-month sentence, which he served at Miramar Naval Brig in San Diego, California.

SUPPORT GI RESISTANCE

Bradley Manning · Colton Turner · Alexis Hutchinson · Jeff Hanks · Rodney Watson · Nicole Mitchell · Eric Jasinski · Marc Hall · Kimberly Rivera · Kyle Wesolowski · Cliff Cornell · Victor Agosto

Pablo Paredes · Suzanne Swift · Tony Anderson · Stephen Funk · Carl Davison · Eugene Cherry · Travis Bishop · Michael Thurman · Ryan Johnson · Brandon Hughey · Katherine Jashinski · Robert Zabala

Mark Wilkerson · Benji Lewis · James Circello · Jose Crespo · Dustin Stevens · Skyler James · Terri Johnson · Ryan Jackson · Ricky Clousing · Carl Webb · Dale Landry · Aidan Delgado

Agustin Aguayo · Blake LeMoine · Robin Long · Diedra Cobb · Chris Capps · Camilo Mejía · Andre Shepherd · Blake Ivey · Joshua Key · Matthis Chiroux · J Hart Viges · Ehren Watada

Design by Jeff Paterson.

Supporters of the first military resister to the Iraq War, Marine L.Cpl. Stephen Funk, join an antiwar march in San Francisco, CA. 10/24/2003

Courage to Resist activists in San Francisco, CA. 10/27/2007

Courage to Resist organizer David Solnit in Oakland, CA. 7/28/2005

Left to right: Buff Whitman-Bradley, objector Robin Long (pg. 105), and Cynthia Whitman-Bradley. 7/17/2009

Supporter Lori Hurlebaus outside of the court-martial of Navy objector Pablo Paredes. 5/12/2005

Veterans for Peace take "Free Bradley Manning" message to the White House. 3/19/2011

Iraq War objectors honored at the Veterans for Peace national convention, left to right, Camilo Mejía, Agustín Aguayo, Stephen Funk, Eugene Cherry, and Suzanne Swift. 8/18/2007

Bradley Manning supporters listen to Dan Ellsberg outside of the Quantico brig. 3/20/2011

Family members of conscientious objector Agustín Aguayo help lead march in Fort Lewis, WA. 2/5/2007

Navy objector Pablo Paredes addresses rally at Canadian Consulate. 1/25/2008

Marchers in San Diego, CA, support Pablo Paredes during court martial. 5/12/2005

Bradley Manning supporter outside of Fort Leavenworth, KS. 6/4/2011

Activists alter messaging of military recruiting center in Oakland, CA. 5/15/2006

March to support GI resistance in San Francisco, CA. 12/9/2006

Rally at the Canadian Consulate in San Francisco, CA, to support U.S. war resisters in Canada. 7/9/2008

Activist supporting GI objectors during rally in Oakland, CA. 5/15/2006

Bob Watada helps prepare for a rally in support of his son, Army Lt. Ehren Watada, who refused to deploy to Iraq. 6/25/2006

Iraq War objector and command rape victim Suzanne Swift upon release from the Army stockade in Fort Lewis, WA. 1/3/2007

Supporters of Suzanne Swift hold vigil near stockade. 2/5/2007

Rural California residents gather to "welcome home" objector Agustín Aguayo following his release from a U.S. stockade in Germany. 5/11/2007

Gulf War objector Aimee Allison speaks out for Iraq War conscientious objector Army S.Sgt Kevin Benderman. 7/28/2005

RESIST

MILITARY RECRUITING FOR IMMORAL WAR & OCCUPATION

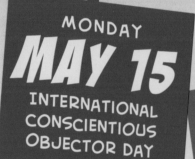

MONDAY
MAY 15
INTERNATIONAL
CONSCIENTIOUS
OBJECTOR DAY

ALSO:
SUNDAY, MAY 14, 2PM
AN AFTERNOON OF SHORT
FILMS & YOUTH PERFORMANCE.
FREE MOTHER'S DAY EVENT
CELEBRATING RESISTANCE TO WAR.
PARKWAY THEATRE
1834 PARK BLVD, OAKLAND

CONSCIENTIOUS OBJECTION IS A RIGHT!

THE WAR IS ILLEGAL. HUMAN BEINGS ARE NOT!

SUPPORT WAR RESISTERS!

STOP THE WAR

4PM RALLY WITH SPOKEN WORD & HIP HOP
OAKLAND CITY CENTER, 12TH & BROADWAY

5PM MARCH TO MILITARY RECRUITING STATION
WITH NONVIOLENT DIRECT ACTION, BROADWAY @ 21ST

COURAGE TO RESIST
WWW.COURAGETORESIST.ORG

OAKLAND

CENTRAL COMMITTEE FOR
CONSCIENTIOUS OBJECTORS
WWW.OBJECTOR.ORG

ENDORSED BY: GRANDMOTHERS AGAINST THE WAR, NOT YOUR SOLDIER, ACT AGAINST TORTURE,
NOT IN OUR NAME, CODEPINK, INTERNATIONAL CAPOEIRA ANGOLA FOUNDATION OAKLAND

Navy objector Pablo Paredes leads antiwar march of thousands in rural California town. 3/25/2006

AWOL U.S. Army war resister Kyle Snyder is embraced by retired Army Col. Ann Wright at the U.S.-Canada border. 8/13/2006

Iraq War refuser Army Lt. Ehren Watada addresses the media.
6/7/2006
Ehren Watada addresses Veterans for Peace national convention
and later faces additional charges due to the content of his
speech. 8/12/2006

Gold Star father Fernando Suarez del Solar introduces AWOL
Army objector Agustín Aguayo at press conference. 9/26/2006

Courage to Resist activists join antiwar march. Air Force objector
Michael Thurman (pg. 127) on left. 10/27/2007

Theater puts the Iraq War on trial during court-martial of Ehren Watada. 2/5/2007

Objector Skyler James, a lesbian soldier denied discharge when outed and harassed, seeking sanctuary in Canada. 12/7/2007

Courage to Resist organizer Buff Whitman-Bradley holds vigil during court-martial of Ehren Watada. 2/5/2007

FREE BRADLEY MANNING

US ARMY PFC BRADLEY MANNING is accused of providing classified information to the WIKILEAKS website, including: ① The *Collateral Murder* video that dep[icts the] killing of at least a dozen Iraqi civilians by a US Apache helicopter crew. ② The *Guantánamo Files* which exposed, among many other things, how the US impris[oned a] journalist known to be innocent of any crime in order to interrogate him about the workings of an international news agency. ③ The *Afghan War Diary*, which d[etails] how US tax dollars are being funneled to corrupt contractors and warlords. ④ The *Iraq War Logs* which, for the first time, outlined the true extent of coalition i[nvolvement in] civilian casualties. ⑤ Scores of embarrassing *US State Department cables*, including those that have fueled democratic uprisings throughout the Middle East.

① No person has been harmed by these releases, yet Bradley Manning faces the death penalty or life in prison for telling us the truth. <u>You can help save his lif[e]</u>

BLOWING THE WHISTLE ON WAR CRIMES IS <u>NOT</u> A CRIM[E]

bradleymanning.org ★ **couragetoresist.org**

Part III:
Looking Deeper
★ ★ ★ ★ ★

It is helpful to think of GI resistance as a spectrum, with many different actions falling within a field of resistance. Each step a soldier takes makes the next one easier. Seemingly small acts of resistance can be one part of a process that leads to outright refusal. For many soldiers, the act of questioning the wars in Iraq and Afghanistan can be a first step in the process of war resistance. This section includes the narratives of those for whom thinking, reading, and talking about the wars were key to their eventual decisions to refuse service.

While on base, troops are subjected to endless amounts of prowar propaganda. From the cadences they are forced to shout in unison, to the TVs blaring exclusively Fox News in the mess halls, to pressure and lectures from the command, troops are saturated in prowar rhetoric. Indeed, this saturation is a fundamental part of Basic Training, as recruits are transformed from ordinary people into soldiers willing to fight and die.

Yet, this environment is not impenetrable. News reports, critical analysis, "inconvenient" facts from outside this propaganda loop have the ability to pierce through this information bubble. The mere act of picking up an article or ordering a book with an alternative analysis of the war can catalyze a new way of thinking about U.S. policy. Likewise, the act of questioning the justifications for the war, or the mentality or orders of the command, can be a first step in a personal process that leads to refusal. The stories of those who refused because of internal processes of education and conscience show that independent thinking can conquer collective brainwashing. The military devotes copious resources into training people to avoid thinking for themselves. Yet, these stories of resistance show that individual conscience and analysis can never be completely wiped out.

Furthermore, these stories demonstrate the power of ideas over human behavior. Through engaging other ways of examining and thinking about the wars, from alternative political analyses to philosophical frameworks, these soldiers were able to make decisions that challenged the ethical framework of the military and drastically altered the course of their lives.

Matthis Chiroux
June 2008

Matthis Chiroux joined the Army in 2002 at the age of eighteen because he wanted to get money for college. He trained as a journalist and spent more than four years writing for Army publications. After he was honorably discharged, Chiroux went to New York and eventually enrolled in Brooklyn College. Soon after that, he was notified that he was being recalled to the military as a member of the Individual Ready Reserve (IRR) and would be sent to Iraq. Determined not to return to a war he opposed, he made the decision that he would refuse deployment.

I enlisted in the military immediately following high school. I did very poorly in high school as the result of being a very depressed young man. I graduated high school with a 2.1 GPA. My family was broke and could not afford to support me going to school, or me figuring out how to go to school after high school. So I enlisted in the military as a way to bridge an uncrossable gap that I saw in my life, from post–high school poverty and mediocrity to actually having a shot at going to school and making a career for myself in some type of profession. The military was offering me money for college, as well as offering me a chance to learn journalism, to learn writing and photography, and travel the world a little bit. So it seemed like a very good option for me, as I didn't have too many others.

Iraq War Looms

I enlisted in 2002. I didn't enlist to "fight the terrorists," or anything that seemed patriotic to the majority of Americans at the time. I enlisted because of the opportunity I saw the military offering me. I didn't really honestly think that going to war was much of a reality or a possibility. I knew we were in Afghanistan. I saw the occupation of Afghanistan winding down. By the time I enlisted, we had pretty much successfully deposed the Taliban, and were more or less occupying the country, and it seemed to me at the time like it was just a matter of that winding down and things going back to normal. It wasn't actually until the week that I got out of Basic Training and I got to my journalism school at Fort Meade that I regained the privilege of being able to watch the news, and I realized that while I was in training there had been a lot of rumbling about a possible war with Iraq. The idea of actually going to war was quite frightening to me as a young man, especially to Iraq, which even then I thought of as likely not having much to do with the war on terrorism. But I just kind of resigned myself to the fact that one way or the other, regardless of my personal feelings, the Army pretty much owned me for the next four and a half years and that I needed to quickly figure out a way to button it up and "toe the line," as they say in the military, and figure out how I was going to survive for four and a half years and not go crazy or not be blown to bits.

I remember, I was still in journalism school when we invaded Iraq and, as I often say, I can remember watching the television and feeling completely shocked and awed as I watched the initial stages of the shocking and awing of the Iraqi people, and wondering, one, how I had gotten myself into this whole mess, and two, whether or not I would be forced to deploy to Iraq and support that occupation—how I was going to do that?

Stationed in Asia and Europe

I was stationed in Japan for two years, during which time I worked for a military newspaper. About the only exotic place I ever went to while I was stationed in Japan was the Philippines. I deployed there for about three weeks in support of a bilateral training mission being conducted with the Filipino Army called Balikatan, and I believe that was in 2005. There I participated in documenting medical exercises, mostly—U.S. and Filipino troops providing free health care to folks out in the countryside in the provinces. And I have to say that mission was quite rewarding to me. I saw U.S. military members working with military members from other countries to do what seemed like a very good and honorable thing, which was take care of people who otherwise wouldn't be taken care of if it wasn't for our presence.

So that kind of repaired my disillusionment a little bit. I felt like, okay, obviously the U.S. military does do some good in the world, and we're not just out there to kill people, but we're out there to help people. I went back to Japan and finished out my time there and then they sent me to work for the four-star general in charge of U.S. Army Europe, Gen. B.B. Bell. I worked in his Command Information Department, helping to produce, edit, design, and lay out *Your Army* magazine, which was their quarterly publication, for the U.S. Army Europe. We were told actually that our target audience was the people in D.C.: the Congress, the president, and the like, to leave them with a good taste of U.S. Army Europe and maybe even a desire to give us more money.

So that was my mission there, and while I was in Europe, I traveled all around the continent. I also went to Afghanistan once to produce a story about U.S. military members from Hohenfels, Germany. They were being deployed to Afghanistan to assist with security in the first parliamentary elections, under the direct command of a Romanian battalion, the Red Scorpions. So I did that story, and then I came back to Germany.

In Afghanistan

While I was in Afghanistan, I saw poverty deeper than I've ever seen it any other place. I saw U.S. military folks seemingly clinging to routine to kill the time and to pass the time until they could be redeployed back to their home stations, which seemed to be the only thing that anybody cared about. I saw fields of poppies and marijuana being grown by the local populations. In fact, going into one of the bases, I got a great photograph of three kids who were trying to sell me hash through the window of the Humvee I was riding into Bagram Air Base. I always thought that was kind of interesting, that I saw us being there to liberate the local population from the control of the warlords who mostly profited through opium production, and I saw the products of that production being offered to U.S. service members. It kind of made me think about stories that I'd heard from Vietnam.

While there, I toured an up-armoring Humvee facility where they were welding giant plates on the side of Humvees to make them armored. I spent most of my time with the four-star general while I was there, so we were treated to a nice and rosy tour of all the wonderful things that were going on—none of which included the prison there at Bagram.

There was a kind of a startling moment: while I was there with this unit from Hohenfels, Germany, I actually witnessed when they told General Bell that only about half of the turrets in their Humvees worked, that the other half were rusted to the point that they couldn't rotate the weapons on top of the vehicles, and that really they were just riding around for show. Were they to come under any kind of attack, they would be completely unprepared to respond. They would have to basically turn these vehicles on the wheels to aim; they couldn't twist these turrets around. The young soldiers of this unit were telling the general about this, and the general was extremely upset and immediately got on a satellite phone and called back to Germany and chewed out one of his guys back there and asked them, "Hey, why do I have soldiers on the ground under the control of this Romanian battalion and their gun turrets don't even work? I want somebody here, fixing these things within twenty-four hours, or you're fired."

What ended up happening was, all of these troops who complained about the turrets got chewed out by their first sergeant and their commanding officer for being whiners and making the unit look bad in front of the general. I think about that specific scenario. I think about that specific situation, and I think about all of the other failures in the wars that this country prosecutes overseas, the failure to get important information passed up the chain of command, documenting failure and documenting deficiency—these things that don't get reported up the chain for fear of looking bad in front of their superiors or fear of making their commanders and first sergeants look bad in front of their superiors.

My fellow Iraq Veterans Against the War are often testifying about the fact that all of these bad things were going on, but that people were failing to report them up the chain because they were afraid of looking bad. They were afraid of being scrutinized as possibly deficient or defective soldiers, as part of deficient or defective units, and that that was somehow *their* fault and they should feel ashamed about that and keep it quiet for the sake of unit cohesion and putting on good appearances for the world and for their commanders.

GI Opposition to Iraq War

While I was in the military, I heard *tons* of opposition among U.S. soldiers to the war in Iraq, and I did from the very start. But like me, most of these people believed that their personal feelings about the mission were irrelevant to their duties as soldiers, and that one way or the other they would have to keep supporting the mission. So there was talk about the immorality of the Iraq occupation, there was talk about the pointlessness of it, but there was never much talk about actually standing against it because most everybody had it trained into them that, well, it wasn't their job and it wasn't their business to be standing for or against any of this, that we were simply paid by the government to follow orders and that anything beyond that was "outside of our lane" as they say in the military, and that we weren't there to address policy. We were simply there to carry out orders.

Civilian Again, Then Recalled

I got out and I moved to Brooklyn, New York. I'm originally from Auburn, Alabama, but I decided that I was going to move to New York City to pursue my education. I got there and I worked a series of odd jobs after arriving in New York, trying to readjust to civilian life. In January I got into school at Brooklyn College. Then in February, I got my recall to the Army. I had it delayed initially. I called them up and they changed my report date from March 8 to June 15. I immediately entered a very deep state of depression. I felt completely alone and isolated from friends and family, living in Brooklyn and not having put down too many roots yet.

I felt completely betrayed by my country. I felt like I had done my time. I served honorably. I kept my mouth shut about things that aggravated me, and, you know, had done my five years and had been honorably discharged, and that I should be now focusing on the rest of my life. I felt betrayed to be having another year of my youth stolen. I was being put in a situation where I was going to be forced to deploy to what I considered an illegal occupation, but I didn't feel I had any choice to stand against it. I locked myself in my apartment and really spun out for about a month—mostly watching and reading news on the Internet and screaming at the top of my lungs and asking questions like, why does nobody care about this? Why do I walk around in the streets and talk about the difference between Sunnis and Shias and people look at me like I'm nuts? Why do I say names like al-Maliki and al-Sadr and people look at me like they have no idea what I was talking about? I was blown away by the fact that even such things as Abu Ghraib seemed to be completely lost on your average American citizen. It really fomented an anger problem in me, and this anger was fueling my depression and fueling my isolation, and I went through a series of very, very low states.

Hooking Up with IVAW

Fortunately, in mid-March, I went to a peace event in Brooklyn where I met up with a number of Iraq Veterans Against the War. This is an organization that I completely agree with about all of their basic points-of-unity. I basically felt like, wow, this is maybe the most intelligent and well-spoken and in-touch group of soldiers that I have ever seen in my life, and they are all speaking of freedom and justice and peace in the wake of having their rights so violated and having violated the rights of others so badly. One soldier in particular really did it for me. Her name is Selina Coppa and she's actually an active-duty soldier who's stationed in Germany, and she was on leave, speaking out against the war in Iraq. She started off with the disclaimer where she said, "The opinions expressed here are my own and not of the U.S. military," and went on to talk about her feelings about the Iraq War.

I looked at that and I said, "Oh my goodness. Here is an active-duty soldier with the courage to speak up and speak out, and then return from leave to uniform and face her command afterwards." I looked at that and I said, "If she can do it, there's absolutely no reason I can't do it. Furthermore, I've been wasting my time with silence these last five years because somehow I had been convinced that I didn't have a right to participate in speaking for peace and justice at all because I had signed away those rights when I enlisted." So many military people believe this is true, and now I have such a good time informing soldiers of what their actual rights are and then pointing them out in the regulations, because a lot of it is jaw-dropping when they realize, "Oh, you mean even as an active-duty soldier I can participate in peace protests as long as they're nonpartisan and I'm not in uniform and I'm not speaking for the Army? I had no idea that was possible."

So I started there. I started going to IVAW meetings, and I started planning an IVAW benefit at my college, which finally came to fruition May 13. And I started speaking on the radio about my feelings concerning the Iraq occupation and why it broke my heart that I would be having to deploy there June 15. Then, right around April, I took a trip outside of the United States, and that kind of cleared my head of our national struggle. I talked to some old friends back in Europe and actually visited my old military base in Germany and spoke to some of my old soldiers and officers about what I was doing with IVAW. I actually found quite a bit of support from all of them, which really shocked me and, furthermore, pushed me one step further to understand, "Hey, the military is full of people who think that this occupation is *really* bad, but feel like they're not able to act against it. But there is really nothing stopping me from acting against it. If I feel this is wrong, I should have the courage not to participate."

Decision Not to Go Back

So I made the decision at that point that I would not deploy to Iraq. In fact, I would leave the country. I was planning on maybe going to hide somewhere in Germany or Spain or the Czech Republic, and hide out until this war is over and war resisters were pardoned and I could come back.

I came back to the United States from Europe, fully planning on leaving about a week before I was supposed to deploy to Iraq, and then I watched my best friend Christopher Goldsmith's Winter Soldier testimony where he talked about his responsibilities—well, he is a forward observer, but while he was in Iraq because artillery wasn't authorized in his section of Baghdad he was turned into the Command Intelligence photographer. And he talks about the photos that he was forced to take and how these photos were not used for intelligence purposes. They were used as war trophies by the noncommissioned officers. And his other experiences in Iraq, and in the military, and going into the military reminded me so much of my own story—including his story of stop-loss and his decision to try to take his own life the night before he was scheduled to deploy—and about his fight to recover from that and to speak out against the war.

Staying and Fighting

I was so moved by the testimony that I decided that not only would I not deploy to Iraq, but I would stay in the United States to face charges if the Army wished to bring them against me, because I didn't feel that it was right for one more soldier to have to go through what he went through, and I didn't feel that it was right for one more soldier to go through what I was going through for a completely illegal cause. It was around *that* that the idea for my personal stand here was forged, and I followed through on it. I stand here a little more than three weeks after having made that announcement, and one week from today being ordered to deploy to Iraq, and I'm still in the U.S. I'm still speaking out against the war.

In fact, I'm lobbying members of Congress. Last week I met with maybe a dozen members of Congress to talk to them about possibly coming out in full support of Iraq war resisters on the basis of the war's illegality. Like I said, if it were not for these Winter Soldiers, these fellow IVAW doing what they were doing and saying what they were saying and taking such a bold stand in the face of—in my personal opinion—the most corrupt executive branch that I've seen in my entire lifetime, that if it weren't for them speaking up and speaking out against that I probably would have skipped the country. But I realized that to leave the country and not force another debate on the illegality of the Iraq War would be a betrayal of the courage of my fellow Winter Soldiers who not only have gone to Iraq themselves but have come back and spoken the truth.

Matthis Chiroux followed through on his public refusal to be deployed to Iraq. On April 22, 2009, he received a general discharge under honorable conditions from the Individual Ready Reserve.

Michael Thurman
July 2008

When Michael Thurman was a junior in high school in 2005, he enlisted in a delayed entry program in the U.S. Air Force. During his time in Basic Training and tech school, Michael began developing strong concerns about the war in Iraq. By the time he was assigned to his first duty station, he had come to oppose the war. He applied for conscientious objector status and after a process that took eight months was discharged as a conscientious objector on June 10, 2008.

In high school, I was really interested in aviation and having a career in aviation. I worked at a little airport, and that field really drew me. So one day the Air Force recruiter came to school, and I was talking to her about joining the military as an aircraft maintenance technician, and then eventually working to become a pilot. It really appealed to me, so I signed up.

That was 2005. I was a junior in high school. I was seventeen years old. At that time I was pretty indifferent toward the war. I didn't care either way. I really didn't know or care about the bad aspects and the reasons for going in. I was young, and I would say kind of naive. I was in a conservative, right-wing household, so I at the same time kind of adopted everything I was being told by our leadership and the news and everything. I guess I was probably motivated purely by self-interest.

All throughout my senior year in high school, I was in the delayed enlistment program. I didn't go into Basic Training until after the summer of senior year. But senior year is when I started to change a little bit. I found some new friends that kind of opened me up to different perspectives and ways of thought—I would say, more of a liberal lean toward politics and things like that. So I started seeing it through those eyes and that's when I started becoming a little discontented with the war and the government, and that's when I started—maybe not totally, but partially—regretting my decision to the Air Force. But I was still ready to go.

Questions Arise during Basic Training and Tech School

I attended Basic Training at Lackland Air Force Base in San Antonio, Texas. After I graduated Basic, I went to electronic principles training at Keesler Air Force Base, Mississippi, and from there I went to my hands-on aircraft training at Sheppard Air Force Base, Wichita Falls, Texas. Then I came back to California, to Beale Air Force Base.

During Basic Training, I questioned a lot of things I was seeing and being taught. They have classes and they teach you about finances and stuff, but they have some classes that are kind of strange. We had one class where they just kept showing us videos—real videos—of people being shot and blown up. I didn't know the point. I guess the point of that class was just to desensitize us. But that's the kind of thing that made me kind of sick, and I started to question what I was being taught. We had chants—one of the chants was about killing people, and it just seemed like a really hateful, angry situation that I didn't want to be in.

I still liked the aircraft, and I was still very interested in aviation, but at that point I was totally discontented with the war and didn't really want to be a part of killing people. But I was already in and I didn't really have a choice, so I just advanced, and I kept telling myself it might get better.

I was a little bit angry about my situation and I got depressed about it a lot. It was actually during tech school where I started studying a lot of Eastern philosophy and thought, and Buddhism and Taoism, and that kind of changed my perspective in a spiritual way toward humanity and toward existence. So I guess I could say at that point I was totally opposed to the situation I was in.

I've had friends who, you know, don't agree with the war and they're always questioning their situation. There are some smart people in the Air Force that I'm still friends with. Most of them just kind of play it off and hope that some day the situation might change, but they're still in the military.

Applying for Conscientious Objector Status

I got out of tech school in May of 2007. My first duty station was at Beale Air Force Base just north of Sacramento, and that's when I started working on the flight line and every day I was out there I just thought of all the indirect killing I was contributing to and I just couldn't take it anymore.

So one day, I told my supervisor that I didn't agree with any of it and I didn't want to be in the military anymore. I told him if there was any way I could get out I'd like to know how. So they took me off the flight line. My supervisor was actually the one who told me about conscientious objector. I actually didn't know the term until I was introduced to it by him.

So I looked into it and I read down the criteria and I thought, "Wow! Yeah, this is what I am, this is what I'm going to apply for so I can get out of the military." So I applied for conscientious objector status. It took me a long time. It was a really arduous process.

They took me off the flight line and put me in an office and I was just doing personnel work, just pushing paper and doing filing. I was like a file clerk. I was still in, contributing to the killing, and so every day I was in constant turmoil—even about the little stuff, like mopping or taking out the trash. It all still contributed to this huge system that I was totally opposed to.

It took a very long time for me to get discharged—eight months from the time I applied for conscientious objector status. What happened was, when I applied I had to write a huge paper about what I believe and how it came to be and why I couldn't contribute to war anymore. At that point, I had to talk to a psychiatrist to make sure I was still sane—I guess they thought I might have been crazy because I didn't believe in war. Then I had to talk to a lawyer at the legal office, and she's actually the one that processed all my legal stuff and determined whether or not I was actually a conscientious objector. Her recommendation to the base commander was to okay my application. I also had to talk with a chaplain. So the chaplain gave me a report about my religious, spiritual beliefs. Then from there it just went up the chain of command. From those interviews the application goes to the legal office on base, and then it just goes up the chain of command, and it went all the way to the Secretary of the Air Force, and it took eight months for that to happen.

Reaction from Others

I actually had some support from some people on my base. They thought if this was what you really want to do, do it. But I did talk to some people that thought I was crazy and didn't really agree with me. But I didn't get hassled that much. No one really went out of their way to bother me or anything like that.

My mother supports me all the way, whatever I did. She supported me when I joined the military and she's definitely supported me coming out. My father, not so much. He thought that I was somehow betraying my country by trying to get out. He wasn't in the military, but he really adheres to the mentality and the doctrine. But eventually he also realized that it's my life and I'm going to do what I want to do with it.

I got discharged on June 10, 2008, and I currently live in Sacramento. I'm about to start going to college here, and I'm going to do some work for Courage to Resist because I think GI resistance is going to be the ultimate thing that stops the war.

Definitely politicians and the government won't do it. It's going to have to be the actions of individuals that bring down the pillars of war.

Tim Richard

August 2008

In 1999, when he was seventeen years old, Tim Richard enlisted in the National Guard in Iowa, hoping to get money for college and happy to be serving his country. In 2005, when his enlistment was nearly up, Richard received notification that his service was being extended and that he would soon be deployed to Iraq. Opposed to the war, he decided to go AWOL and head for Canada.

My father was born in New Brunswick, up in Canada, and my mom was born in Andover, which is near Stonehenge of England. My dad went to university in Prince Edward Island. My mom was in the Royal Navy, and they met there. My mom left the Navy and they moved to California, and that's where I was born.

I first got a call from a recruiter when I was sixteen and I knew my grades weren't good enough to pay for university, and this was about 1998. They were offering a lot of benefits and it was the National Guard. I thought we would be doing disaster relief, and that sort of thing. So in 1999 in November I joined. I was living in Sioux City, Iowa. I signed up for six years and I went to Basic Training. That's pretty much how I became involved with them.

Basic Training and AIT took about seven or eight months because I signed up for communications—fixing radios, fixing computer networks, that sort of thing. They had actually promised a lot more money to me when I joined. But when I was done with advanced training, they told me about some laws that had changed in the State of Iowa, so the amount of funding they were actually giving me was being cut in half.

I was supposed to do the one week a month, two weeks in the summer thing, and I really enjoyed what I was doing. I liked the idea that I was able to go to school and serve my country at the exact same time.

Questions about Iraq War

After 9/11, just like just about any other American, I kind of wanted a piece of something, especially me being in the military. I wanted to do the right thing. I wanted to go get whoever who did this to America. I was behind the Iraq war when it started because I had thought it had to do with 9/11. But after the Iraq war dragged on for a bit, then I realized that there's no weapons of mass destruction in Iraq; there's nothing but poor people and a lot of dead bodies. So I started doing some research on the war and I realized that, well, there's basically a bunch of bull that has been fed to us. I'd been thinking about becoming an officer, thinking about making a career out of the military. But I decided that at the end of my six years, I would just get out of the military. I had to say six years is enough. I'm not going to re-enlist. I don't want anything to do with the Iraq war.

I started asking questions; I started talking to people with different perspectives on some things. I learned about the full President Reagan–Donald Rumsfeld connection to Iraq—how

Saddam Hussein was installed to counter the Iranian Revolution, which came about because of the U.S.-installed puppet Shah in Iran. I started realizing that the root cause of all of these things was basically the U.S. That really got me thinking about what's the point of even being there. I also started thinking, well, is military intervention and killing people in this manner right? I mean it's one thing if you're defending yourself, but if morally I just really had problems about the idea of going into a foreign sovereign country, invading and toppling the leadership, taking their resources, and killing people. To me, that was a huge moral dilemma.

I'd say the moral misgivings were much stronger than the political misgivings because like I said, I joined the military with the idea of defending the United States and I would, if that had been the case, I might feel differently about the Iraq war. But now I just felt like what they're asking me to do was just flat wrong. Shooting somebody who's virtually defenseless is wrong and that's something that I didn't think I could be any part of.

Stop-Loss

In about August of 2005, our unit got a warning saying that some members would be deploying to Iraq. They had told us when we had joined that they don't break up units, they don't send individual soldiers. If you go, you go with your unit. But it turned out once the Bush administration had got done with us, that was simply not true because they kept using us to populate other units that were going over to Iraq. I was a few months from getting out of the military when I got a warning order saying I will be deployed to Iraq. I asked, "What about my contract?" and they said I was Stop-Loss. I found out later, after I cut to Canada, and after I had got hold of my personnel file, that my contract had been extended from November 23, 2005, to December 24, 2031!

I read the paperwork. You know, everyone said, "Oh, you signed the contract; you'll just have to deal with it." That's not in the contract. No one tells you about it when you sign up. So as far as I'm concerned what they did is illegal, but the Supreme Court of the United States held up that they're allowed to Stop-Loss. This all means there's really nothing you can do in that situation.

Well, I knew they weren't going to keep me for that long—2031—I mean, that's silly. They're not going to keep me for twenty-five years, I don't think. That was my thinking at the time. So, I decided that I would deploy to Iraq. They pulled me out of my unit, which was a cavalry unit, in which I was fixing radios, and they started training me with an Infantry unit along with communications duties, training me in regular Infantry duties such as house raids or defending convoys, and that sort of thing.

Decision to Go AWOL

I decided around November of 2005 that this is just ridiculous. I cannot morally do what they're asking me to do. By deploying to Iraq, I felt like I'd be a liability because there's no way I could shoot somebody who was simply trying to defend their own home from a foreign invader. They did all these mock training exercises. We were in full battle gear and we were raiding mock houses, with actors yelling at us in Arabic and that sort of thing. I had blanks in my rifle, and during the exercise I "shot" two unarmed civilians with the blanks in my rifle. It annoys me thinking about it. I don't know if anyone even saw me, but I realized at that time that, if this is Iraq, those people will be dead. All they were doing was trying to defend their home. So I almost threw away my rifle and ran out of there.

I sort of coordinated a plan. I decided that I'd wait a few days and on November 23, 2005, the date my original contract was set to expire, that's when I went AWOL.

They were training us in Mississippi, and we were under lockdown. Lockdown means that you can't go anywhere without someone knowing, not even the bathroom. You had your rifle with you. You had your uniform on at all times, but because November 23 was Thanksgiving, they had decided to cancel training for the day. They let us wear civilian clothes and lock up our rifles, and they decided that they were going to bust into the town to go into Wal-Mart. They said, "Oh, by the way, we'll just drop you off in town. Have fun. Come back in nine hours. We'll pick you up." So I figured, if this isn't a sign, I didn't know what was.

So I got onto the first bus I could, snuck away from the main group. I called my mom. I didn't tell her exactly what all was going on, but she bought me a plane ticket from New Orleans to Seattle. So the plan was to get to New Orleans, take the plane to Seattle, cross the border in Seattle to Vancouver, then meet my mom where she was living in British Columbia at that time. Well, that's a short version. That's what I did.

My heart was pounding the whole time. I was sweating. I was so paranoid because it really takes only one phone call, one person to realize what you're up to, and your name goes in every computer—military, FBI, local police, everything. It doesn't take that much these days to have people looking out for you.

So, I mean, I tried to alter the way I walk. As soon as I got to New Orleans, I threw away my dog tag. I threw away my military ID. I tried to act normal. I tried to do the best that I could to sort of blend in. Of course, the haircut sort of gave it away.

Crossing into Canada

When I got to the Canadian border, I basically had a one-way car rental. I had an out-of-country drivers' license from the U.S., four hundred dollars cash. So I was thinking, "Okay, I'm busted." My plan was to get out of the car and start screaming, "I'm a Canadian citizen!" and let them … let them not kick me out until they figure out my situation. But the border guard was really nice and said, "All right, have fun. Welcome to Canada," and that was pretty much it.

My father's a Canadian, so I could apply right away for citizenship. I'm glad I did not claim my Canadian citizenship earlier, because if I had claimed my Canadian citizenship as a child, the U.S. military would have made me forfeit it upon joining the military. When I came to Canada, I was able to go ahead and fill all the paperwork, everything, basically sit on my hands for about eight months and wait for the citizenship card to come in. Now I'm a full-fledged Canadian citizen and I've got the same right to privileges as every other Canadian citizen.

War Resisters Support Campaign

I'm working up here with the War Resisters Support Campaign. Here in London, Ontario, we've got a local chapter and right now we care for four war resisters here and we've had ten others pass through. We do fundraisers, a lot of political lobbying, a lot of talking to the public, that sort of thing. I try to be as active as I can with the group, to help the resisters who come up here. In some ways I feel really guilty because, you know, just because I'm a Canadian citizen, just because my dad was born in New Brunswick, I somehow have a privilege they don't, and I don't think that's right, that I have a privilege that they don't, simply because of where my father was born. I've done the exact same thing they've done, and in fact, I think what they did is a little bit more courageous because I came up here knowing I could get Canadian citizenship if I didn't get arrested at the border. These guys that come up now, they've got no claim to Canadian citizenship. They don't know what's going to happen to them. So that's why I try to work and try to be as outspoken as I can about the War Resisters Support Campaign.

Having the war resister background but also being a Canadian citizen, I like to think of myself as sort of like a bridge between the two groups, between the Canadian peace movement and also the war resisters.

Matt Mishler

Matt Mishler was a twenty-four-year-old Marine reservist from Orlando, Florida, when he realized that he could not, in all good conscience, participate in war. With that realization, he made up his mind to apply for a discharge as a conscientious objector. When he announced his decision publicly, Mishler said that he would go to jail rather than deploy to Iraq or Afghanistan.

When I signed up, I was twenty years old. I was at a real cross-roads in my life. I wasn't really liking the job I was in. I wasn't in school at the time, and growing up I'd always thought that it was everybody's duty at some point in time to serve for their country. Kind of naive as to what that really entailed, I just thought that it was everybody's duty to serve their country, and at the time I thought that was what I wanted to do with my life. I decided to join the Marines because I heard it was the hardest boot camp. So that was my thinking at that time. I don't think I really put in the thought that I should have put into it before I even signed the contract.

I looked at it as a challenge. Going through boot camp, I graduated platoon honor man—number one in my platoon. I was very motivated at a certain point in my military career.

From boot camp we had combat training, which was about a month long, and then more school in North Carolina. I was there for four or five months. So in all, I was on active-duty status with boot camp and everything for about eight to nine months. After that, I returned to my home in Michigan and then I moved to Florida in December of 2005 to join the reserve unit here in Orlando, where I did one weekend a month and two weeks a year.

Troubled about Dehumanization

I started to realize that my train of thought was not common among other Marines I was around. The way that they would talk, I would kind of distance myself from the talk-paths that they would go down. I didn't really voice my opinion so much, but I didn't want to hear about people saying ignorant things, like, "Oh, I can't wait to go kill some 'hajjis.'" I found it very appalling and very ignorant. I started thinking: these are people; they have a mother; they have a father; they might have a family—they're not just "hajjis" or whatever you want to call them. They were brought up in a different situation than we're brought up in, and they're brought up with different beliefs—who's to say that you wouldn't be that person that you're pointing your rifle at if you were brought up in the same situation.

I've read a lot of literature and my religious beliefs and my moral beliefs have really come together. Even if you go back to World War I or World War II, a lot of people in a combat situation weren't even able to even fire their rifles, but come Vietnam, the number drastically increased because the military started using tactics to dehumanize. I mean, I remember even through boot camp we used the word "kill" like it was nothing.

You use it to acknowledge commands: "Kill, yes sir. Kill." But…it couldn't change my opinion of people: that they really are people. Just because they don't agree with me, that's a human life, and in Jesus Christ's teachings, I don't see where he would ever condone the killing of another human being. I try to live my life as much as possible through the Sermon on the Mount. A lot of people say, "Oh yeah, yeah, that's good to read, but you can't live your life by that," but I think why would Jesus Christ say those things if that's not exactly how you're supposed to live your life. So that became very strong in me. I didn't want to dehumanize humans.

Even in combat training, there were video games… but war is not a video game: you kill someone, they don't come back to life; they're dead. And that was a person that probably had kids, has a mother, has a father, probably has a wife, has obligations, they have a life that they're living and you just took it upon your own judgment to take that life. I don't think that should ever be upon another human being; I think that's up to the Lord and the Lord only, and not up to any one human being whether a person should live or die.

Beliefs about Killing

Going through the conscientious objector status process, they ask you a lot of questions: "Well, what would you do if we had a situation like Hitler?" It's hard to say what you'd do in that situation, but how do we know what really would have happened if we didn't do anything? Because we had a lack of faith in God, and an abundance of fear, we acted on it, but how do we know what really would have happened if we would have put our faith in God knowing that God would take care of us.

But this war in Iraq to me is a very easy war to decide on, that what we're doing is morally and religiously wrong. I've heard stories of Marines who have mistakenly killed civilians. If you look at the Christian "just war" theory, that civilians should be no part of a war really—and we're just totally ignoring that. This war…it just seems so easy to me to see that we're stepping in places that we shouldn't be stepping in and making decisions on people's lives that we shouldn't be making.

I remember when I first handed in the paperwork, my commanding officer even said to me, you know I'm going to make sure that I point out to anyone that's going to be reading these documents that I don't think you should be a conscientious objector. Then I had another conversation with a sergeant major and he said that I'm basically ruining my life. But when you look at that, me ruining my life in my opinion is going to be different from what the sergeant major believes is ruining my life. What he believes is ruining my life is getting out of the military and looking at possibly getting an other-than-honorable discharge or a dishonorable discharge. But to me, it's a test of your beliefs and your faith, and I have enough faith in God that if I can't get a job because of my military career then I was not meant to have that job. I don't put a job before my faith in God, and I don't put the military before my faith in God either. When you have to choose between either of those two, it's clear-cut to me that you have to choose your faith.

Dealing with the Consequences

It comes down to your beliefs and how strong your faith is. But to me, I'm not defined by my job or anything else; I'm defined by my faith in the Lord and my faith in my religion. If it comes down to "Well, either you're going to Iraq or you're going to have to spend time in the brig or jail," then that's what I'm going to have to do to serve my God. That's what I'm going to have to do, because I don't see serving my God and doing God's word as picking up a rifle and slinging it over my shoulder and walking through Iraq or Afghanistan and shooting other people.

I've said it to the classes I've spoken to too. You know, I've thought about me having my rifle pointed at another person and him having his pointed at me—would I really want to make that decision and pull that trigger? And if I did, how would I feel after taking that person's life? Was that really up to me? That's a decision that I refuse to make, and I feel so strongly in that belief that I would rather do jail time. I would rather do anything possible than to be put in a situation where I would have to choose another person's life over mine because I don't see my life any more valuable than another person's life.

After a process that lasted several months, Mishler was granted CO status and honorably discharged.

T.J. Buonomo

November 2007

*T.J. Buonomo is a graduate of the U.S. Air Force Academy
and a former commissioned officer in the U.S. Army. He was
discharged from the military not for refusing to fight but for
expressing his political views to fellow officers. Today, he is
an active member of Iraq Vets Against the War.*

Every year between a half dozen and a dozen cadets from each
of the service branches may choose to commission into another
branch. So I, along with about a dozen of my fellow cadets,
decided to cross-commission into the Army instead of the Air
Force. My reason for doing that was because I was a political sci-
ence and Middle East studies major and also had an Arabic minor,
so I thought the Army could probably put that to better use.

Studying the Reasons for War

Between my junior and senior year at the Academy, I started
doing a little bit of reading about how we got into Iraq, because
I'd heard some things about prewar intelligence and some of the
controversy surrounding that. So the first book that I picked up
that really exposed me to all that was James Bamford's *A Pretext
for War*, and that laid out everything about the weapons of mass

destruction controversy and some of the disinformation that laid the basis for us going to war with Iraq. So at that point, I basically did everything I could to find out as much as I could about this issue, and just continued to study it and research it throughout the rest of my time there at the academy and on into the beginning of my career in the Army.

In the academy, they always stressed leadership and integrity and ethical decision-making, so reading this book helped me understand the Constitutional issues involved here. According to the Constitution, it's Congress's responsibility for declaring a state of hostilities with another country—and therefore they require accurate intelligence in order to do that. In the case of Iraq, it became very apparent that that was not the case. So it presented me with a very serious ethical dilemma.

I decided that, at that time at least, I would continue to study and to train and prepare to go over there. At the time I thought basically that, okay, maybe they rushed into this, and proper decision-making was not carried out, but, you know, we were still there to bring democracy and freedom to the Iraqis.

E-mail Discussions with Other Officers

I started to discuss via e-mail some of the more controversial issues about not only prewar intelligence, but also the U.S. government's involvement in drafting this law, which would allow American oil companies access to the Iraqi oil industry, which continues to be a very controversial subject. So some of them would ask questions and they would ask me to back up some of my sources in defense of my arguments. They mostly refrained from offering opinions themselves because they were aware of the possible repercussions of voicing dissent.

Eventually, one of the recipients of my e-mails was becoming very uncomfortable with some of the things I was writing about these issues, and began, I think, to question in his own mind my loyalty. So he forwarded all these e-mails to my commander. I was called into my commander's office and eventually they began an investigation into some of my statements—verbal and via e-mail—and, after a month of investigation, came to the conclusion that I would not be fit to deploy.

Probably the most controversial statement in their mind was expressing my support for the impeachment of the vice president, because I viewed him as one of the central architects behind the disinformation campaign that led us into Iraq, and also him being behind this effort to give U.S. government control over the Iraqi oil industry.

Released from the Army

Article 88 of the UCMJ [Uniform Code of Military Justice] states that officers can be punished, as criminals essentially, for making what's termed as "contemptuous statements" against higher-level public officials.

I was never threatened with a court-martial. It certainly was a possibility. But they chose to pursue administrative action. I don't know exactly why; I wasn't privy to their internal discussion on this investigation. But I think that if they would have chosen to pursue a court-martial, that would have opened up a very difficult case for them to pursue and also the serious issue of the right to free speech. They pursued it administratively and that kind of allowed them to avoid that potential problem.

I have some mixed feelings now. I was scheduled to deploy to Afghanistan around maybe January of 2008. I didn't have a problem with that; that was fine. Afghanistan to me was a very different war from Iraq. I think we had legitimacy and justification to go into Afghanistan. Iraq was a completely different issue. But I would just say that I'm also very disappointed and very disillusioned with our government right now, because of my personal experience and reading about the experiences of other people who have voiced dissent throughout the government. My experience has been that your political loyalty is essential to your serving in a government position, and that is not how it should be, and that is in fact, I think, setting a very dangerous precedent. There have been numerous accounts of well-qualified people in higher positions than mine who have basically been excluded from the decision-making process.

Joining IVAW

I'm currently involved in Iraq Veterans Against the War. We've been planning for an information campaign to educate people on how we got involved in Iraq and what is currently going on behind the scenes, factors that are contributing to the violence there. Basically, we want people to know that the violence in Iraq is not going to end until the occupation ends, because the occupation is fueling it. People aren't going to stop resisting it until we leave. Our soldiers, our troops, are being killed there. Innocent Iraqis are being killed because the political situation there is constantly in flux and you have all these factions fighting for power there. By continuing to involve ourselves in a process that they need to figure out really for themselves, I think that we're just really perpetuating this conflict.

Military Officers Speaking Out

Officially, speaking up about illegal policies and actions is what we're supposed to do. That's what we're told. But unofficially, it's a very different story. It's a difficult thing. There are difficult decisions to make, and all you can really do is make those decisions based on the best information you have. What's really important, I think, for anyone who serves in the military or the government is that you seek out that information. I think, throughout our government, there are a lot of people who would rather not expose themselves to some of these controversies and who would prefer to remain ignorant of things that could cause them to have to make a moral decision. That is another serious problem. We need people who can really think for themselves and weigh the facts and make the best decision they can no matter how difficult a decision it is.

Ryan Jackson
April 2008

Ryan Jackson joined the Army in 2005 and after Basic and Advanced Individual Training spent a year in Korea. While there, he began to develop misgivings about what the military does to service members and about the war in Iraq. By the time he returned from Korea, Ryan was determined to get out of the Army. In late 2007 he went AWOL for three months, and in early April 2008, Jackson turned himself in at Fort Sill, Oklahoma. He was sent from there to his base at Fort Gordon, Georgia, where he was court-martialed and sentenced to military prison.

I was a mortgage loan officer before the Army and got tired of working a lot of hours, and basically just joined the Army to switch careers. A lot of times, it's difficult just to go to college, take out the loans and then you're in an entry-level job anyway and you owe all these student loans at the end. So initially for me it was just to switch careers and switch into the IT communications field, and I ended up going into satellite communications in the military.

When I joined, I wasn't really in agreement with the Iraq war. I guess I was indifferent; I didn't really feel strongly one way or the other. I thought, you know, I might go, I might not. The other benefits and things that they offer seemed more important or more enticing at the time.

A Year in Korea

After Basic Training I went to Fort Gordon, Georgia. I went to school there for about eight months. Then for my first duty station I went to Korea for a year. Fortunately for me, Korea is not currently a combat zone. I enjoyed the Korean culture and the Korean people and I liked Korea, but I started to really see the Army for what it was and what it did to people. I started to see that the Army is run in an authoritarian way where people are just kind of like robots. People would just do whatever they were told, whether it was morally right or whether legalities were correct, even disregarding their own beliefs and morals. People just start to become drones.

Also, I started to see people that maybe had family problems, or had things going on at home—family members that were sick or deathly ill—and we had some training exercise so the Army wouldn't let them go home to see their family. I started to see that the Army doesn't really care about you as a person. Once you are no longer of use to them, that's when they won't care what you do, and then they'll be eager to get rid of you. They try to preach that your family is important and everything else is important and the Army takes care of you, but at the end of the day I came to the realization that you're just a number to them.

Also, while I was in Korea my original beliefs, not really agreeing with the Iraq war, started to more fully develop. I started to research civil rights movements, and research history. I started to watch documentaries, and it just started to evolve and build and build.

Confused about What to Do

I came back from Korea and went on leave for a while. I actually started to try to talk myself out of leaving the Army, trying to say, "I need to do the right thing, and I need to be patriotic, and I need to stick this out and serve out my time." I even went to a Special Forces briefing. I told myself that... "So I'm going to do the challenge... I'm going to be the complete opposite. I'm going to try to go Special Forces and try to convince my mind to just keep going." Because you are the minority if you speak out, and they have a way of trying to make you feel like you're worthless.

That thought—the Special Forces thing—had started to evolve at the end of Korea. Then I went on leave and I said to myself, "Who am I fooling? I cannot ignore my morals or my conscience, and it would be morally wrong for me to do that." So I started to research further and then progress from there.

I looked at people back in history such as Henry David Thoreau and Gandhi and Martin Luther King, and different civil rights leaders, people back in the old days that faced real persecution and were chastised for their beliefs. I came to the conclusion that these people did this before me, way back in time, to fight for civil rights and fight for peace and nonviolence, and it really started to change me. It really started to evolve, and I said, "Well, who am I in today's age when we supposedly have this freedom, and the worst case they're gonna do to me is possibly imprison me for a little bit but I'll still be alive to tell about it another day."

Small Acts of Resistance

I had never been in any trouble in the Army. I always did a good job. But once I knew that I had to do something, that I could no longer support this organization, the Army, I started to build up negative reports from my superiors. I wouldn't come in the morning for PT, I'd come in at eleven or noon and leave early. I was doing this on purpose, and I told them I was doing this on purpose to get enough negative evaluations that they could just administratively discharge me.

When I got to the point where I was almost out, I had a company commander who told me to my face that he was going to make it as hard as possible for me to get out, and that yeah, I'd eventually get out if I keep going down the path, but it wouldn't be on my terms.

Going AWOL

Right before New Year's Eve of 2007, my company commander was trying to get the colonel's approval to put me in pretrial confinement. That's when I left. I stayed in Georgia for a couple weeks and then I went back to Detroit, where I'm from.

My mom is a strong conservative Baptist and has the Republican mind-frame, and believes that "you enlisted and you should stand up to your word" and so forth. My dad was more understanding, but I think they were both a little disappointed that I didn't finish it out. I think my dad was more receptive. I just told my parents that the fear of not being able to live with myself was greater than the fear of not living. It's inevitable in the Army that you would go to Iraq or Afghanistan. I knew that I had to do something before I got put in that situation, because I knew I would flat-out refuse.

Finding Support

I had looked online and had been researching. I had read a lot about IVAW and about Courage to Resist online. I was looking for lawyers, and I had called different lawyers. It was real important to me to find a lawyer that had the same beliefs as me. I knew if I wanted to really fight this, I needed one that firmly believed that I have the right to believe what I believe. A lot of lawyers wanted $200 just to talk to them, just for a consultation, and I didn't have the money to waste $200 just to hear an initial opinion.

When I was researching online I actually stumbled across some message board about turning yourself in at Fort Sill—for people that have gone AWOL from Basic or AIT. On that message board I found an attorney, James Branum, out in Oklahoma. I talked to him for a while, and through his encouragement I decided that I was going to go out to Oklahoma where he was, try to turn myself in at Fort Sill, and see if they would just process me out there. But when I got to Oklahoma and I met James Branum, I ended up not turning myself in for three or four days, because I started to really bond with him.

I actually did a little bit of speaking there with a Mennonite church that does peace and social justice work. These older people do a peacekeeping meditation on Fridays and I spoke to a group of them and told them my story. I got really inspired by these people who were just almost in tears telling me how moved they were and that they needed more young people that wanted to stand up and they'd like me to come back out to Oklahoma and talk to high schools. I always did sales work before the Army, so it's just my natural ability. I just had a kind of knack for that kind of work. But it was always just to make commission in the past, part of my job.

I guess my Oklahoma trip really changed my life. I started to believe, like, this is kind of my calling. Now I don't have to try to convince people of something just to make commission; it's coming from my heart. I felt like it's so much easier to talk to people and tell people about something that I'm not trying to make money off of, just something that I firmly believe in. I started to talk to these people and realized that there are a lot of other people out there that share the same beliefs as me, people like Camilo Mejía, and other war resisters before me that have faced other things and inspired me. I just felt like no matter what the Army decides to do, if I just take that and turn it into a positive experience, and use my story and what I have to say to hopefully other people, maybe save one person from going to kill other people or possibly get killed themselves, then the sacrifice I've made I feel is worth it.

After he turned himself in, Ryan Jackson was court-martialed, sentenced to a hundred days in military prison, and discharged from the Army.

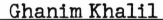

Ghanim Khalil

December 2007

Ghanim Khalil joined the U.S. Marines when he was eighteen, because he had no way of paying for college. He served four years active duty from 1995 to 1999. While he was in, he served as a Muslim lay leader at his base. He completed his four-year active-duty commitment and was discharged honorably. After that, he spent two years in the Inactive Reserves, and then he joined the Army National Guard. In February of 2003, in the lead up to the invasion of Iraq, Ghanim held a press conference at which he went public with his opposition to the invasion and stated that he would, if necessary, refuse deployment. He was honorably discharged from the National Guard several months later. Since he got out, Ghanim has written a book titled Contemplating Dissent: Why Saying No to the War in Iraq Was the Right Thing to Do from a Muslim Point of View.*

I joined the Marines for financial reasons. I wanted to attend college, and I couldn't. So I thought it would be a good deal if I signed up with one of the services in the armed forces. I happened to just pick the Marines. I liked being a Marine, but I wouldn't say that I fit under the category of gung ho.

I liked the training. I liked the fact that I met people from all over the United States from different backgrounds. But there were aspects also that I didn't really relate to. Certain subjects were discussed that I didn't really agree with, chiefly concerning our role as a nation in other nations or in other regions. I read up on a lot of our history, foreign policy history. You hear Marines talk about other people or other countries in a very generalized way, where they put down an entire people, because, you know, the Marines were in that country, like for example, Lebanon—a lot of Marines hated Lebanese people because of the barracks bombing. But that didn't really make sense to me, because it's different to study Lebanese people on one hand and then our involvement in the country on the other hand. It doesn't make sense to generalize and hate all Lebanese people because of the barracks bombing.

Anti-Muslim Bigotry in the Military

Regarding anti-Muslim bigotry, a lot of the Marines that I was with, they didn't really have too much of a working knowledge on what was really going on outside of the United States concerning our foreign policy, especially where the military's involved. During the four years I was in, between 1995 and '99, the Embassy bombings happened in Africa, and that again resulted in negative attitudes toward me because I'm a Muslim and toward other members of the Marine corps that were Muslim. So there was some tension going on. Also tension when everyday things happened. I used to pray. When I prayed five times a day or when I fasted during the month of Ramadan, those things kind of excite the curiosity of certain people who begin to ask questions and then when they find out other things, they kind of suspect foul play because I'm a Muslim—what am I doing in the Marines, and stuff like that.

The harassment was more like comments made here and there, not about me personally but about Muslims and Islam as a religion. A lot of the comments are comments that people make when they're drinking or comments people make after reading the news or watching the news on TV. It wasn't directed personally to me, but it was comments that were made about a people, about my religion, that are offensive to me because they're either racist or they're just ignorant.

Because I was a lay leader, I had a connection to Washington, D.C. Washington, D.C., endorsed me as a lay leader and so that connection I had with Washington, D.C., kind of made some people not want to talk to me or say too many things in front of me. But other Muslim Marines that I knew, and people in the Army that I knew who were Muslims, they went up against a lot of things that I would call straight-up discrimination.

A Switch to the National Guard

It was 2002 when I joined the Army National Guard in New York City. I did that for two reasons. One was because of the talk about unilateral action toward Muslim countries, and the other was the drum-up to the war on Iraq, and I thought I'd have better chances in the military if I switched from Marines to Army, especially the National Guard. My view of the National Guard at the time was that they guard the nation, they stay in the United States during times of crisis. Of course that's false. You know the National Guard gets deployed as well as the regular Army reserves and active services. But thinking that they would stay in the United States, and I could end my eight-year contract within the National Guard, I switched over to the National Guard, because I was Supply Administration in the Marines and even if you're in active reserves, they always need supply people. So I thought maybe it would be better for me, with my views, to switch over into the Army National Guard.

Going Public with a Press Conference

In the year 2002, when the drum-up to the war was happening, I became really concerned about that. In the Marines I used to study U.S. foreign policy. I used to study military history. I read from a lot of different viewpoints, so I was in touch with a lot of knowledge from different perspectives. In 2002, when I was in the Army National Guard, when I'm hearing all this drumming up to war, and I'm familiar with a lot of what our policy is toward the Muslim world, especially people we don't like or know nothing about, I suspected that this was really a plan of the neoconservatives to kind of get control of an area that they consider important, that they consider vital. So I spoke to a lot of people within the military and outside of the military about how to properly address the situation of mine. I didn't want to go to war. I didn't want to be part of an attack on a country for reasons other than defending the homeland, to be involved in something that I considered grossly unconstitutional.

So I was given options. I was told, maybe you can switch into an MOS [military occupational specialty] that doesn't get deployed, or maybe you can become a lay leader for Muslim people again and assist the chaplain. But those choices were really not solid possibilities, because you could still get deployed with any of those reasons. In February 2003, I contacted Citizen Soldier. The director is Todd Ensign. He's someone who's been working with military people and vets for a long time, and between him and me, we thought the best option was for me to have a press conference, because trying to resolve my situation within the military hadn't worked. I went to a chaplain; I went to my staffing COs [commanding officers]. The best thing, the safest thing for me—and I really, I really care about the principles here—the safest thing for me was to have a press conference to let the military know how I feel, to let people, the American people know how a soldier feels, or how a former Marine feels and then see what happens from there. That's why I held the press conference, because I thought, I can't keep silent.

I knew the war was going to happen. I wasn't one of those people who thought maybe this thing is going to go away or that diplomacy is going to win out. I knew the war was going to happen, because the war had started six months prior, with the bombardment, and some people knew that. So that's what led up to the press conference, and the press conference is where I said, "These are my reasons, one, two, three, a, b, c, why I think this war is illegal and immoral and I don't want to be a part of it. I think it's unconstitutional."

One reason why I did the press conference is because when I went to the chaplain, he mentioned Stop-Loss. He said it was likely that my unit was going to be under Stop-Loss. So I was thinking, "Oh, I only have like four months to go and I'll be discharged honorably, and this guy's talking about Stop-Loss," and I knew the war was going to begin before I got discharged. I felt speaking out would be my only way out, or at least people would know that some soldiers feel this way.

Support from Other Soldiers

When I came back to my next drill after the press conference, a lot of the soldiers congratulated me, and one of them said, "I wish I could do the same thing, but I can't because I have a family and I've been in for this amount of years, and it would just be a bad move." But a lot of them agreed with what I did, and they didn't really harass me or really put me down. The only person who did put me down was a sergeant who was a former Marine and he did that only because there was a picture in the *Daily News*, the *New York Daily News*, of me in the dress blues, in the Marine Corps dress blues. I didn't wear my uniform at the press conference, but they used a picture of me in uniform for the story, and he hated that, you know, a Marine was on the *Daily News* saying the opposite of what Bush was saying, and my message contradicted the president. He hated that because he thought it made the Marine Corps look bad, and he had very harsh statements for me. But other than him, a lot of the people, a lot of the members of the military, they either didn't talk to me or they congratulated me and supported me.

As far as the community's concerned, nobody really opposed what I did. My neighbors didn't. My friends didn't. And I started going to some of these peace groups, local peace groups, and they supported me, and I met a lot of fine people.

I was due to be discharged May 9, 2003, and I made my statements February 15, because I knew the war was going to be initiated before that, and I knew that it was likely I was going to be deployed in it. But because when I did the press conference I was not in uniform, I didn't break any laws. I just stated what my views were. They really can't act against you if all you're doing is just stating your views and you're not in uniform. So there were no regulations, no laws, no rules that I was breaking. And the war happened. My unit didn't get deployed before May 9. And so the natural thing for me was to get discharged honorably, because I didn't really break any laws or rules or regulations. I just spoke my piece.

Addressing Racism

After my press conference, I got a chance to know a lot of people, a lot of veterans and peace groups. So a lot of the discourse within those peace groups was about the immoral policies and why unilateralism isn't the right thing, and how America's turning into an empire or is an empire already and stuff like that. But when it came down to discussing the role of the other, in this case the Arabs or the Muslims, the history of the Middle East or stuff like that, they didn't really have too much of a knowledge about that. So what I did was I tried to communicate about how Muslims are ordinary people. Americans misunderstand a lot of the things that Muslims do—what their religion is about—and I tried to fill those gaps in, but the way I was going to do it was within an antiwar context. I was going to talk about why it's important for the antiwar movement to know what Muslims are like, to humanize Muslims, because that would make their job easier to educate Americans about how war is not really the right way. I think the policy within the military, when it comes to the ordinary soldier, is that you shouldn't have any remorse for these people. They're the enemy; do your job. When it comes to the policy that's informing the military, I think it is very racist.

In my book I don't only concentrate on American distortions about Muslims. I also have to talk about how Muslims misunderstand Americans, because all they see is missiles and tanks and President Bush on a television before war happens. So it's a dual thing, and I think that's important to mention.

> *Brandon Hughey needed his father's signature to enlist in the U.S. Army as he was only seventeen years old at the time. Like so many other young people, Brandon was hoping to get money for college by signing up and serving, but he began to have misgivings almost immediately upon entering the Army. After he completed Basic Training in November of 2003 he was sent to Fort Hood, Texas. By then, he was determined that under no circumstances would he allow himself to become complicit in the illegal occupation of Iraq. Rather than remain in the Army, Brandon traveled to Canada, seeking refugee status in that country.*

I was called one day at my home by a recruiter. The first thing he asked me was, "Do you have a way to get to college?" I said, "No, I haven't really thought about that." So he said, "Well, stop by our office and we'll talk about it some time." So we made an appointment. I stopped by there, and he told me all the other wonderful things that they could do if I just enlisted for a few years. You know: pay for my college, pay for a signing bonus, and basically cover everything. So to me, it sounded like a good deal at the time.

I thought it would be a good move to jump-start my life. I was just coming out of high school and didn't know what I wanted to do and didn't have a way to get to college. I thought I'd be doing good things, signing up to defend my country and fighting for the right causes. That's the image I had in my head—I was gonna be a good guy.

Second Thoughts in Basic Training

I started to have second thoughts in Basic Training because I sort of felt like I was being reprogrammed to think differently than what I'd been taught my whole life. But at the time, I just thought those thoughts were normal and that every soldier has them, so that the best thing to do would be just to put them in the back of my mind and continue on and just get through it.

I began to notice that it was not just teaching people how to fight, but it was also completely dehumanizing the other side. It was a lot of racial slurs, a lot of insults that are just commonly used toward Arab people and toward Iraqi people. You began to see that they don't think of them as equal. They think of them as less than us and it seemed like they tried to drill that into our heads, that they're not as good as us and they're less than us. I suppose they do that because when you're over there it makes it easier to point your rifle and kill them.

I'd been taught that all human life regardless of country of origin is of equal value. Just because somebody's from Iraq or the Middle East doesn't mean that their life is worth less than an American. In Basic Training you began to notice that they sort of didn't share that way of thinking, to put it lightly.

I figured that if I said anything about that it'd just make me a target, and the best thing to do would just be to get through it. If I still felt like I was having second thoughts then maybe I could talk to my new unit about it once I got out of Basic Training.

Expressing Misgivings to Superiors

When I got to Fort Hood, I began to talk to my superiors about my second thoughts. I told them that I didn't think what was going on in Iraq was the right thing to do. You know, when I signed up I had this image that I was going to be defending my country and fighting for the right reasons, and when the war in Iraq started I began to feel that that wasn't so. We had attacked a country that never threatened us, and basically laid waste to the entire country, and they'd never done anything to us. So I'd expressed my thoughts about that, and the reply was, they told me to stop thinking so much. I had also been promised a signing bonus in my contract and my recruiter told me I would receive that after Basic Training. I did not, so when I asked somebody about it they told me I should be more concerned with doing my duty than with the money I was being paid. So it seemed that a lot of things weren't the way that I thought they would be when I signed up. When I expressed those thoughts to my NCOs I tried to get a discharge, and they told me that there was no way that was going to happen.

So I went AWOL for the first time in January 2004. I stayed AWOL for twenty-eight days and then came back before the thirty-day cutoff to see if maybe they would boot me out. I thought once I go AWOL, once I've shown that I'm not a "good soldier," maybe they'd just boot me out. So I came back after twenty-eight days and instead of kicking me out of the Army they said, "Well, we're glad to have you back; we're going give you extra duty and dock your pay, but I suggest you pack your bags and start getting ready to go to Iraq." So basically that idea had backfired. I had tried to get myself booted out, even *that* didn't work. So at that point I began to feel like I was trapped, that there was no way out.

The Canada Option

Basically, I began to think of what other options I had to get out of the military. I couldn't really think of anything. I tried going AWOL and coming back. At that point I just felt trapped. I had remembered that tens of thousands of people had come up to Canada during Vietnam. I thought at the time, well, maybe as a last resort I can leave the country. So I kept that in the back of my mind. When I realized it didn't seem like any other way I could get out, I began to feel that, okay, leaving the country is my only option. At that point, I began to make plans to go to Canada.

I was just going to pack my bags and drive myself there, try to set aside whatever money I could and hopefully have enough to get myself started in a new life and a new country. I didn't really have much of a plan because I didn't know what I was getting into, but that was pretty much it. I came up in March of 2004.

I was staying with a Quaker family for a few months when I first arrived. The Quaker community did a lot to support me. That was really my first support network when I came to Canada.

Support from Family and Friends

When I was leaving I made the decision not to talk to my family until I actually crossed the border. When I came to Canada, I called my dad and told him that I was here. Obviously he was quite shocked, didn't really understand why. But after a couple weeks we talked, and after he got over the initial shock he sort of came around, and he's been fully supportive now.

All the family members that have contacted me have been supportive. I talked to my mom and my brother, so most of my immediate family is supportive. It's nice to have that because

I know some of the guys up here, their families don't support them—some of them have even disowned them. So I am pretty thankful that they've been behind me through all this.

I've had e-mail contact from a few of my friends in high school, and most of them are supportive. Most of them want to come up and visit me some time whenever they can.

The only part that's really bad about being in Canada is I can't visit my family when I want to. But they can come up and visit me. Other than that, Canada's a great country with great people and if I'm able to stay here and make my home here I'll be completely thankful.

Concerns about Deportation

We appealed the denial of our claim for refugee status to the Supreme Court and they basically said they wouldn't hear the case, and they didn't give a reason why. They didn't say anything about it. We checked their website and it just had one word after it, "Dismissed." That's all the information we got from them. Why they refused to hear it we don't know, but that was that. Once they said no, there's nothing else we could do about it.

At this point they can deport us if they choose. They just have to send out a Pre-Removal Risk Assessment form, you fill that out, send it in, and any time after that they can issue you deportation orders. So theoretically it could happen any time now.

I do feel nervous about it, but you just try to live with it and hope things will change, which it looks like there may be a possibility of something happening soon. We're pretty excited about the Immigration Committee of the government of Canada. It's made up of members of Parliament, and each party has a member on the committee based on how many seats they have. One of their members put forward a motion to set forth a provision that would let U.S. deserters stay in Canada, and the committee voted on the motion and it passed seven to four. The four votes against it were all Conservative, and the seven for it were the three other opposition parties. But basically they passed the motion, and it now says that the Immigration Committee supports a provision to let us stay here. So basically now that committee has to take that provision forward to Parliament and they'll vote on it there, and if it passes in Parliament then basically we'll be allowed to stay here.

Position on the War in Iraq

I think as the war goes on longer, more people are beginning to see the same way we do, and although everybody might not necessarily support us, I think a lot of people even in the States are beginning to realize that the war in Iraq is a hoax. The reasons given were completely false and we invaded a country that never threatened us. We're not using our armed forces to defend the country; we're using them to push around people who've never done anything to us. We're killing them and we're doing all these horrible things, and for what? The more people come around and the more pressure we put on the government, hopefully one day we can stop it.

Brandon Hughey still lives in Canada. There has been no final decision by the Canadian government about his case.

Part IV:
Resisting Military Abuse
★ ★ ★ ★ ★

There are some who refuse service because of abuse and degradation they suffer while in the military. It is difficult to capture the extent of mistreatment within the ranks, because it is so woven into the fabric of military life. Racism, sexism, and homophobia are endemic to the military, with recruits regularly suffering harassment and discrimination. The military imposes a contradictory culture of building up camaraderie between recruits while utilizing divide and conquer strategies of racism, sexism, and homophobia to keep people in line. Discipline is imposed through clear hierarchy and tight control, leaving little room for individuality. Troops are deployed again and again to the ongoing wars in Iraq and Afghanistan, and are often denied the medical and psychological care to recover from previous deployments.

The military is built around a deeply macho culture, where female recruits are routinely referred to with derogatory names and berated by the command, as well as other recruits. A 2004 study published in the journal of military medicine found that 71 percent of the women were sexually assaulted or raped while serving in the military. The problem of sexual assault has recently gained new visibility with high-profile stories published in the *New York Times* about women, in the field of battle, who avoid going to the bathroom at night because they are afraid they will be raped. As a result, several women died of dehydration.

The military is also a deeply racist and homophobic culture. Historically, people of color who have served have been given more dangerous jobs at lower pay. Today, people of color are disproportionately recruited, and once in the military, suffer from a culture that directs racism toward them, as well as the enemy. Under "Don't Ask, Don't Tell," LGBTQ people are forced to hide their sexuality. Those who express a nonconventional sexuality or gender presentation are often berated, harassed, and beaten up, while the command sits idly by or takes part in the abuse.

The military uses fear and intimidation to prevent recruits from speaking out. Boot camp is designed to erase individuality and incorporate the new recruit into the "chain of command." Within the military, it is hard and scary to speak out about mistreatment. Those who do so are often informally punished by the command, through public ridicule, ostracism, and intimidation. This can prevent many from complaining about mental and physical healthcare needs or abuses they are suffering.

We are seeing troops being exhausted and used up from multiple and lengthy deployments, with large numbers suffering from PTSD. This goes hand in hand with systemic practices of denying troops the medical and physical care they need, and sending them back to war even while they are still recovering from the previous deployment.

This section includes the interviews of service members who have refused to fight due to severe mistreatment they have experienced at the hands of the military. Their testimony demonstrates how the military contributes to its own undoing.

Suzanne Swift
February 2009

Suzanne Swift joined the Army in 2003, having been assured by a recruiter that she would not be sent to Iraq, but her unit was ordered to deploy almost immediately after her Military Police training. Soon after arriving in the Middle East, Suzanne had to deal with the sexual advances of superiors. One of those superiors coerced her into a sexual relationship. After returning to the States, she was due to deploy again but chose to go AWOL instead. After her arrest and court-martial, Suzanne was discharged from the military in 2009.

I don't know, honestly, why I joined the Army. They had a really good recruiting pitch and I didn't have anything else to do. They gave me a job where they said I wouldn't deploy to Iraq, which I thought was a really great thing.

I went to Fort Leonard Wood in Missouri for Basic Training and for MP training, and after that to Fort Lewis, Washington, for three, maybe four weeks before I went to Iraq. It was kind of a whirlwind.

Sexual Advances from a Superior

We were still staging in Kuwait and I had a platoon sergeant proposition me for sex, and I was completely in shock. These people are supposed to be like your parents, especially when you're brand new, a brand new young soldier. It's really appalling that someone would do that.

I told him no, and then I told a couple other people that it happened and just sort of put it out there to see if I could get any advice. I ended up talking to the equal opportunity representative about it and he said that he would talk to the commander and figure out what to do about it. But nothing ever came of it, ever. The propositions from him stopped, but another superior began to make advances.

From Kuwait we went to Karbala, Iraq. There I was basically coerced into a sexual relationship with my superior. He was my squad leader, in a staff sergeant position, an E5. It went on for months, and when I tried to end it, he used every resource he had available to make my life miserable, to punish me for it.

He'd tell me the wrong times to be somewhere and then punish me for being late or not being at the right place. Just do little things that would make me look bad. He'd spread rumors about me and make me look bad in every possible way and then would punish me for looking bad. Once the punishments began, he stopped his sexual advances.

I didn't report it officially, but I told a bunch of people—everybody knew what was going on and nobody wanted to fix it. With the way that he was treating me, he made it look like I was just a bad soldier. So even if I had reported it, he could have just told them, "Oh, well, she's mad because I punish her. She's making it all up." I kept my head down and tried to stay out of trouble.

More Trouble in the States

Once we got back to the States, I moved to a new unit that was standing up and I had a squad leader who didn't proposition me for sex but would say little nasty things to me. He was my team leader and he would call me at night and be like, "Oh, what color panties do you have on?" or "What are you doing right now? Oh, you just got out of the shower, so you're naked right now?" It was nasty. He was just a crazy little creep.

And I did report him. I had been through enough and I was, "You know this guy is not getting away with it."

I reported him to the equal opportunity representative, and he did his job for once and took it up higher to the commander. They did an investigation during which they accused me of sleeping with him and gave me a class from my commander on how to prevent sexual harassment from happening to me. The man who was harassing me got a very harshly worded letter of reprimand. But that was it.

I was pretty angry, but they moved me away from him so I didn't have to work with him, which is what I really wanted.

Going AWOL

At the beginning of 2006, I was ordered to redeploy with my new unit, but also with the first guy who sexually harassed me—the one that first propositioned me for sex. He was there. At first I just mentally prepared and started packing my bags and dealing with everything I needed to deal with and then eventually when the time came, I just couldn't do it.

I was at my mom's house. I was getting ready. I had my keys in my hand and I was saying goodbye to everybody and I looked at my mom and I said, "I can't go back there. I can't go back to the place where there's no one to help you when something bad happens." If my squad leader then had decided to do the very same thing, I would have been absolutely helpless.

So I just didn't go. For a while, nothing happened. I got some phone calls from the Army and I just turned my phone off and stayed at a friend's house in southern Oregon and kind of hid out.

Then on a Sunday night I was visiting at my mom's house and all of a sudden there are flashlights in my face and cops knocking at the door. It was pretty scary when they took me to jail. Three days later the AWOL Apprehension Team came to get me from the county jail and I went back to Fort Lewis.

Back at Fort Lewis, they just put me back in my unit. They tried to put me back under the same guy. My lawyer, actually, threw a big fit about that and got me moved almost immediately. So that was good.

Then the Army decided to court-martial me and in the meantime gave me a job working at the Provost Marshall's Office filing cases.

My court-martial was about six months later. They charged me with AWOL and missing movement. Eventually I pled guilty to them. There was a whole long drawn out battle for that, but I got a summary court-martial where they gave me the max for reduction in rank and also the max for jail time, thirty-three days, but they didn't take any pay, which was nice.

I actually served twenty-three days. I went to jail for Christmas and New Year's and I missed my sister having her baby.

When I got out, I went back to Fort Lewis and I had a really hard time there. They gave me orders to go to a new school for a new MOS [military occupational specialty], which was part of the deal and to go to Fort Irwin after that, which I did. I was at Fort Lee in Virginia, doing training, and then I went to Fort Irwin. That's where I spent the rest of my time.

It was actually a pretty decent ending. I won't say that the Army was awesome at Fort Irwin, but... it's more of a garrison environment so they really like to crack down on the things that get overlooked in the rest of the Army, you know. So as far as sexual harassment goes and command wanting to really crack down on that, they were great. I reported something that I saw that wasn't even happening to me and there was a huge investigation. And the guy, even though they didn't find any proof, the guy got moved to a new unit and I think whatever happened is on his permanent record. I mean, like they really jumped on it.

I got an honorable discharge, so I didn't lose my VA benefits. I was pretty upset about the whole Army thing at the time, all the harassment was happening, but it actually turned out pretty good.

Dustin Che Stevens
May 2009

Dustin Che Stevens joined the Army immediately after high school because he saw no other alternatives for himself. In Basic Training, he began to have panic attacks and other emotional problems. In spite of his repeated attempts to get out, the Army wouldn't let him go. After Basic, he went to Airborne school, but at his graduation ceremony sat down on the field and refused to participate. After meeting with his chain of command, he was told to go home and wait for his discharge papers. The papers never came, even after Stevens called to inquire about his status. Seven years later, he was stopped for a minor traffic violation when the police discovered an outstanding federal warrant for his arrest. Today, Stevens is on restriction in Fort Bragg, North Carolina, having been told by the Army that it plans to court-martial him and send him to military prison.

I was eighteen when I joined the Army. Basically, I came from a kind of broken home. I had two parents that were recovering drug addicts and it just seemed like a way out. I did it blindly, without even thinking.

After I started Basic Training, I just started having panic attacks and anxiety attacks and, I mean, I just didn't transition well mentally into the military. I told them on numerous occasions that I didn't think it was right for me and they just kept telling me, "Suck it up, everybody goes through it, you'll get better when you get to your unit, it's just the breaking-down period." But I never recovered from it while I was there, and on the day of graduation I told them that I didn't want to graduate, that I just couldn't do it anymore, and that I was sorry. Our first sergeant told me there was two ways I was leaving, one was to graduate and one was in handcuffs and that scared me a lot because I didn't know how the military worked and maybe they could lock me up for not wanting to finish Basic Training. I found out later that that wasn't the case, but I was scared at that time so I went ahead and graduated.

Airborne School at Fort Benning

Then I went to Fort Benning, Georgia, for Airborne school and it was more of the same. I was having panic and anxiety attacks and started to have blackouts and didn't know what to do. So they recycled me my first week of Airborne school and sent me home for two weeks saying that maybe if I went home for a little bit that I would get back in the mindset of the military. So I agreed and I went home.

While I was home my father got me in touch with a psychologist, Dr. Paul Adams, who was a Quaker. He's deceased now. I started talking to him about how I would freak out and when and in what situations. He gave me some literature on conscientious objection and I started reading it and started thinking for myself.

I knew in my heart and in my mind that I couldn't kill anybody. I couldn't be a part of an organization that did so. I went back and I told them that and they said again, you're going to jail if you don't finish. So I finished Airborne school and kept in touch with Dr. Adams, and on the last day I told him, "I'm not going to graduate." He said, "Do what you feel is necessary."

Refusal to Graduate

So at Airborne graduation, I sat down in the middle of formation and refused to graduate. They pulled me off to the side and asked me what my problem was and I told them. I said, "I'm tired of getting the runaround. I'm telling you I have a problem. I have it documented that I have panic and anxiety attacks and I'm refusing to do my duty. I don't care now if I go to jail. If you're going to send me to jail I'm willing to take it because this is what I believe in and I'm not going to fight."

I was scared. I said I was willing to go to jail or die for my beliefs, but it's scary to face that. It made me proud and scared at the same time. Well, they took me to the side and let everybody else graduate and they said that I would be an entry-level separation, and they were going to keep me away from everybody because they didn't want morale going down. They said that they'd send me home and I'd await further orders. So I agreed to that and I went home. I paid for my bus ticket and I went home. I never in seven years received any orders. They'd overpaid me for a month, and I received bills for that and I paid it back. But that's all, that's the only bit of information I got from them.

I called Fort Benning once and they said there was no record of me at all. And I said, "Well that's weird, I went through Airborne school there." I told them my story and they said, "If you're an entry-level separation we take you out of the system, so there probably wouldn't be any record of you." They said I didn't exist.

A Surprise Arrest after Seven Years

After that I went about my life. I've had several jobs, and had background check after background check to get jobs. I started working at FedEx, and they do a federal background check. I've been pulled over numerous times. Stayed in Louisville, Kentucky, the whole time, paid my taxes. I've had a car, paid car insurance the whole time, had a license. So it's not like I've been hiding.

I was leaving FedEx one night driving home and got pulled over for my tags being expired. So the police officer pulled me over and said that my tags were only five days expired so he'd just write me a citation. He went back to the car, and was back there for a while, and then four more cop cars whipped up and they all had their guns drawn, telling me to get out and lay on the ground. I didn't know what to think. The cop that pulled me over told everybody to calm down, that I hadn't shown any aggression at all.

So he let me sit up and he had me handcuffed at this point and he told me why they were doing it, and I started crying because I didn't know what was going on. He told me to calm down. He said he'd been in the military before and asked me if I had a DD214. I said, "What's that?" and he started laughing and said, "That's your discharge papers." I said I'd never heard of those before. He was very nice and he told me that they'd probably figure it out whenever I got to where I was going and they'd probably just discharge me, and he said he was sorry.

In Limbo at Fort Bragg

So I went to county jail, and I was there for five days. They had a federal warrant for my arrest for desertion from the military.

They let me out of jail on my own recognizance and gave me two days to get to Fort Bragg, North Carolina. So two days later I went to Fort Bragg. Upon arriving, I didn't see anyone except for the first sergeant there, at eighty-second Replacement Attachment, which is where I'm stationed right now. He told me that somebody would talk to me within the next couple of days. But I arrived on the first day of a four-day weekend and I didn't see anybody for four or five days.

The person I talked to said it usually takes two to four months and that I was going to probably be court-martialed. If I couldn't provide a DD214 I was going to be court-martialed and tried by JAG officers for desertion or AWOL and probably sentenced to jail. There was no "maybe you'll beat it." It was more or less, "If you don't have a DD214, you're going to jail."

There are probably sixty of us in this barrack right now and all of us have different stories. Some guys went AWOL after going to combat, some guys left—nobody there left like I left—but there's a lot of guys that left during training, right after training. It's just a mix of people. One thing that we've all seen is there have been guys coming in and their urinalysis test comes up that they're full of drugs and they've gone AWOL numerous times and they get chaptered out with no jail time. But most of us are in a kind of limbo state. We don't do anything all day and we don't know what's going to happen to us.

The best way to describe walking into where I'm at right now is, if you've ever walked into an animal shelter, all the dogs that run up to the cages and want to leave. That's the look on all these boys' faces that want to get out of this place. They let us off for the day, and we're allowed to go within fifty miles of Fort Bragg and guys come in beat up all the time, drunk, crazy, crying, doing, I mean, trying to commit suicide. I've seen that a lot and it's crazy.

If you go to a doctor here and you tell them you're depressed, they just pump you full of pills. A lot of these guys try to overdose on them. I've seen that numerous times. There's a guy that is supposed to be on suicide watch that's attempted suicide four times. If you're supposed to be watching him how is he doing this four times?

It's a feeling of nothingness, like you can't do anything to get out of it no matter what your story is. The prosecution lawyer flat out told us we're all going to jail. He didn't sugarcoat it at all, he said I'm sending you all to jail. The last couple of guys from here to be court-martialed, one guy got two years and the guy after him got fifteen months. He was a Purple Heart veteran and had PTSD. He was diagnosed with PTSD by more than one doctor, but the lawyers took his Purple Heart and sentenced him to fifteen months with a dishonorable discharge. I was only in the military for a little under five months and they're threatening jail time and a lot of guys are getting a year. My military career was only five months. I might go to jail longer than my military career was.

I'm not a bad person. I'm not a criminal. I've seen criminals tried for all kinds of heinous crimes and not go to jail. My only crime was that I quit a job and didn't do the right paperwork, and I wasn't told otherwise. I just want everyone to know that I'm a good citizen and I just want to take care of my family.

Dustin Stevens was finally discharged from the Army in the fall of 2009.

Jose Crespo

June 2008

> *When Jose Crespo came back to the U.S. on leave from his deployment in Iraq, he returned to some serious problems confronting his mother and sister. Crespo requested help from the Army with his family problems and got none. Feeling he could not leave his mother and sister, Crespo stayed home rather than return to Iraq. About a month later he turned himself in at Fort Carson, Colorado. Working with a lawyer, he tried to secure a hardship discharge or a posting near his family so that he could provide the help they need. The Army's response was to order him to fly back to Iraq. Crespo refused. This interview was conducted on June 11, 2008, two days before Crespo was scheduled to return to Iraq.*

When I was in Iraq, my grandmother died and my family called my first sergeant and they denied me leave, you know, to go to her burial. So I accepted it because I couldn't do anything anyway. Then my first sergeant came to my room and said that he would do everything in his power to make sure that my family knows of their condolences to her and to apologize that I couldn't be there and they were going to send some flowers. When I went home, I found out that none of what my first sergeant said ever happened: they were never sent any roses, no flowers; they never sent a letter; they never talked to my family after they finished with me, telling me all these things—that they were going to give their condolences and they were going to send flowers and everything. So that's when the trust issue with me and my chain of command died.

Serious Emotional Problems at Home

As soon as I came back on R&R [rest and recuperation] leave from Iraq to New Jersey, I found out about my sister and my mother. My sister's been in the hospital because she tried to kill herself. My mom was still struggling with her, so I stayed home with them until they got better. I took leave I wasn't supposed to, so technically they've said that I was AWOL for the simple fact that I took more of the leave than I was supposed to for the condition that was in my family. I just didn't trust my chain of command to help me with this since they lied to me about sending flowers for my mom due to my grandmother's death and all that.

Right now, my sister, she's been in the hospital twice for major depression, and my mom also had severe anxiety and depression and two people who are sick cannot take care of each other. They asked me to help them with the situation, and I agreed to it, to help them and try to be as supportive and help them in any which way or form that I can. Due to the fact that I'm single, I have no kids, I'm able to do those things. My sister was recently diagnosed with bipolar disorder and schizophrenia and you really need to monitor her and make sure that she's okay. The thing is that my mom works because she has to pay the bills at home and she also needs to take care of my sister, so it makes it difficult for her to do it on her own. She asked me to help her with that if I can, and I told her I would do everything in my power to try and help her and try to see if the Army would help me to try and help her. But they haven't done anything yet. I've showed them documentation and everything on my sister and on my mother—all the things that's happening with them and all that—and they haven't helped me.

Seeking a Discharge

I've requested a hardship discharge, and also a compassionate action, which is me being stationed near my home so I can be able to take care of them and we're able to work something out.

I was supposed to go back to Iraq on April 12, 2008, but I stayed home to take care of my sister and to make sure my mom was okay. I came back to Fort Carson a couple of weeks later, well, almost a month later. May 12, 2008. I turned myself in to them. When I got here they had no charges on me, so the MPs let me go. So I came to the barracks and they put me on LOS, which is "line of sight." The next morning, I presented the issue to my chain of command. I told them what was going on. I told them I came to face the responsibilities of what I did and everything, and I told them what was going on with my family and everything, and they didn't seem to care. All they cared about was sending me back to Iraq. Then after that, I was able to get a hold of some counselors, and they were helping me with the rules and regulations on when you have family issues.

They've denied me leave. They're trying to fly me out on Friday. Right now we're in the process of doing an Article 138. My chain of command here and my chain of command in Iraq right now know about my situation. They have all the documentation needed to approve the emergency leave and the hardship, but they are denying me for the simple fact that they said that they don't want to help me, that I'm needed over there, and that the mission comes first.

Right now, I'm not sure what I'm going to do. Right now, we're talking those things out. We're just waiting on the Article 138, and if that doesn't go through then we'll just take things a different way I guess. It all depends on the situation and how we're going to deal with it afterwards.

Jose Crespo did not go to Iraq. He was given an honorable discharge in September 2008.

Skyler James

August 2008

In 2006, at the strong urging of her family, Bethany Skyler James joined the U.S. Army in spite of opposing wars in Iraq and Afghanistan and being an out lesbian. After a year in the military, suffering ongoing harassment because of her sexuality and hearing gruesome stories about Iraq and Afghanistan from returning vets, Skyler decided she'd had enough and, with a soldier friend, went AWOL to Canada where she has lived for the past year. She spoke to Courage to Resist from her new home in Ontario.

Well, I joined the Army because my parents thought it would be a really good idea and that I'd get travel out of it and get all this experience under my belt. So I didn't want to let my parents down, so I went ahead and did it. This was back in October of 2006.

It did cross my mind that I might be going into a combat zone, but I wasn't thinking about it too much.

In Basic Training, I was being ridiculed for being an out lesbian. I was vaguely familiar with the "Don't Ask, Don't Tell" policy. When I joined, I thought that it wouldn't be that big of a deal and that I wouldn't get found out.

There was one incident that really caught, that really still stings in my mind. I was in AIT, and I was coming back from the bowling alley and somebody ran up behind me screaming and screamed out, "dyke," and the next thing I know I got punched in the back of the head. I didn't report it because it was like a week until graduation. I didn't think anything was going to be done.

The Motor Pool at Fort Campbell

After AIT, I was assigned to the motor pool at Fort Campbell, Kentucky. I was a mechanic there. At first, there wasn't any harassment. I was the only female in the motor pool in the entire battalion and that really freaked me out, 'cause they would always . . . they would claim me as one of the guys, but then after they found out that I was gay, they completely turned their backs on me.

I tried to get one of my sergeants to let me talk to the first sergeant about being a homosexual and having homosexual conduct and whatnot, and he told me flat out, "No, I will not let you talk to the first sergeant about it."

I was there for a year, and during that time I began to think about leaving the Army. I was just getting really tired of being ridiculed. I was receiving hate letters on my door, threatening to injure me and come into my room at night and kill me. So I had a talk with another soldier who was in the same battalion, and we both decided that it would be best for us to leave.

Opting for Canada

Soldiers who had returned from deployment were everywhere at Fort Campbell, and they would always talk about what they did to the people over there in Iraq—these are horrible things, and I thought, "Why are they bragging about them and trying to one-up each other?"

We were told that we were being deployed to Afghanistan, and we made a really, really quick decision. It was a Friday night, and my friend approached me about it and said, "Do you still want to go up north?" I had no idea what he was talking about, so he had to clarify that he meant Canada. So we got in his truck and loaded our belongings into it and just drove away.

We came into Windsor, Ontario. We were heading to Montreal, but we kind of ran out of gas at Cornwall. When we crossed the border, at first they said, "We need to see your passport and birth certificate and blah blah blah." We were like, "Well we don't really have that." He said, "Well, just show us your military IDs." Then he asked where we were going, and we told him that we were visiting Toronto, because we knew that they had a big war resisters campaign there.

We didn't get in touch with the War Resisters Support Campaign right away. We were just getting a feel for Canada. It was really, really exciting. Then, when we ran out of gas, I was like, "You know I think it would be a really good idea to call them now."

They're very helpful. If we had not contacted them, we probably would not be where we are right now. I'm allowed to work in this country, and I am. I have a job. I have a nice little apartment and so does my friend, and we're both really happy.

Uncertainty about the Future

Well, when I first came here and my family found out, they were really upset. They wanted me to come back like right then, and I had to make them understand why I couldn't. It wasn't only that I didn't want to go back and get arrested; it was the fact I didn't have any money. I couldn't go back even if I wanted to. They were really, really upset about everything, but my mom came around, and she supports me now. She still wants me to come home, but she's like, "I want you to be happy." And my dad is undecided yet.

I wouldn't want anybody else to have to go through what I faced personally in the military, and I don't agree with the "Don't Ask, Don't Tell" policy. My sexuality has not been an issue at all up here in Canada. They've welcomed me with open arms.

In my opinion, my case could go either way. It's like a pendulum, like on one side of it, I'm relaxed and I'm enjoying a very comfortable lifestyle, and then on the other side I could be deported at any time, and I'm freaked out.

Skyler James is still living in Canada awaiting a final decision on her application for refugee status by the Immigration and Refugee Board.

Part V:
Collateral Murder, WikiLeaks, and Bradley Manning
★ ★ ★ ★ ★

The Courage to Reveal the Truth

An Interview with Daniel Ellsberg about WikiLeaks, Bradley Manning, and Official Secrets

by Buff Whitman-Bradley

On April 5, 2010, the whistleblower website WikiLeaks posted a video dubbed Collateral Murder *(www. collateralmurder.com). The video, taken from the gun camera of a U.S. Apache helicopter and complete with a chilling "soundtrack" of the comments and conversations of crew members, showed unarmed Iraqi civilians (one, a photographer working for Reuters, was carrying camera equipment) casually walking along a Baghdad street when those in the helicopter began firing. The panicked civilians tried to run and hide from the gunfire, but there was no escape for the dozen who were mercilessly slaughtered by the Apache's 30 mm cannon. When a van drove up and those inside tried to rescue the wounded, the helicopter fired on the vehicle as well, even though two children were clearly visible in the front seat. The children were injured but did not die.*

The video caused an immediate international uproar, with denunciations of the massacre and calls for an investigation. The Pentagon did investigate and found no wrongdoing on the part of the helicopter crew. In addition, the military probed the leak itself and, not long after, named twenty-two-year-old PFC Bradley Manning, an intelligence analyst serving in Iraq, as the whistleblower. As soon as it became known that the Army had identified and detained a suspect, Courage to Resist joined with many individuals and other organizations to form the Bradley Manning Support Network to raise legal funds and organize public support for the young soldier and to help him find a civilian lawyer. Manning was originally imprisoned in Kuwait but, after much pressure from his supporters, was transferred to the Marine Corps brig in Quantico, Virginia. He has retained a civilian defense attorney, David Coombs of Providence, Rhode Island, and as of this writing is awaiting trial. If convicted, he could face life in prison, and possibly, execution.

Since the posting of Collateral Murder, *WikiLeaks has published thousands of pages of classified material about the wars in Iraq and Afghanistan. In July 2010, they released 75,000 documents pertaining to the war in Afghanistan; in October 2010, nearly 400,000 concerning the war in Iraq; and in December 2010, more than 250,000 secret State department cables.*

Whether or not it turns out that it was Bradley Manning who released the video and the other documents, it seems safe to assume that the whistleblower, whoever he or she might be, hoped to have an effect on U.S. policy and to help bring about an end to the wars in Iraq and Afghanistan by making public the mindless brutality of what the U.S. is doing in those countries—the military misconduct, the torture, the senseless slaughter of civilians, the lies, and the cover-ups. That is what America's most famous whistleblower, Daniel Ellsberg, was hoping to accomplish back in 1971 when he leaked a secret Department of Defense study of the war in Vietnam, the infamous "Pentagon Papers," to the New York Times. *In the following interview with Courage to Resist, Ellsberg talks about his reaction to the WikiLeaks revelations, about the courage it takes to risk life in prison to reveal government secrets, and about the role of WikiLeaks in a society with what former CIA analyst Ray McGovern refers to as "the Fawning Corporate Media" so eager to print government lies and so reluctant to print the disturbing and violent truth.*

[Editor's note: Since this interview was conducted, there have been many developments in the case of Bradley Manning and of WikiLeaks founder Julian Assange.]

Buff Whitman-Bradley: Let me set the context for this interview. This is for a Courage to Resist book to be published in 2011 called *About Face*, in which members of the U.S. military who have refused to fight in the wars in Iraq and Afghanistan talk about what led them to take that risk. Some of them became conscientious objectors, some of them have gone AWOL, some have fled to Canada, some have been captured, tried, and imprisoned. In thinking of these resisters, we realized that what Bradley Manning is accused of doing is another form of resistance—revealing classified information, blowing the whistle on government cover-ups and lies. What WikiLeaks is doing by publishing those classified documents is also a form of resistance. It's that kind of resistance we want to talk with you about. So let's begin by talking about the WikiLeaks video that they called *Collateral Murder*. It showed the slaughter of a dozen unarmed civilians just walking along the street in Baghdad. I would imagine that you, given your history, would have had a pretty strong reaction when you first learned about the leak of that classified video. Can you talk about what your reaction was?

Daniel Ellsberg: I can't remember exactly when and how I learned about it. But when I did learn about it I looked up the video and watched it, and of course it is very powerful. I saw both the shorter version and the longer version. And very obvious to me, for example, that whatever the questions, whatever the thoughts may have been in the minds of the people in that Apache helicopter as they started, it should have become very clear in the course of that thirty-eight minutes or eighteen minutes that what they were doing was a war crime when a wounded man who turned out to have been a Reuters photographer and who had been carrying a camera that they somehow mistook for an RPG [rocket-propelled grenade] had been wounded and was now crawling for help to get away in the street. Clearly unarmed, clearly wounded, he was in a situation where ground troops were on the way, I believe were within blocks at that moment, with an ability to capture these people even if they were seen as enemies. To simply shoot down an unarmed person in a case where you could take him into custody is murder. It's a war crime and it's a crime of murder. After all, not all killing in war is murder, but some of it is. In fact, a lot of it is. That was a situation which to me as a former company commander, platoon leader, operations officer, training officer for a battalion, it was very clear to me that that was the sort of situation that was defined as one where you had no right to be killing that person. So that I think the description of it as collateral murder is appropriate, although the "collateral" is in question.

BWB: In addition to the content of the video there was the fact that this war crime, this evidence of a war crime had become a classified document and was leaked. You're probably the most famous whistleblower in America, so did you feel some affinity with the person who leaked the video?

DE: Well, I saw it as something that should have been leaked. I was already aware that Reuters had known about the tape and had been trying to get it for almost two years through FOIA [Freedom of Information Act] and had been refused. The reasons for refusing it were clear enough, namely embarrassment, strong embarrassment, to the military. But they're not legitimate reasons from the point of view of the regulations or of democracy and freedom of information. So clearly this was the right thing to have leaked and the right thing for WikiLeaks to have released it.

I quickly felt, with Bradley Manning identified as the accused source of this, from what he's reported to have said to Adrian Lamo and in chat logs, I felt an immediate identification with him, specifically with his saying that he'd seen things that were almost criminal. I would say that "almost" is a euphemism here. I think they were clearly criminal in this particular case, and probably in other instances he was looking at. He mentioned in those chat logs another massacre even larger, which has not yet been released but which he said he had given to WikiLeaks.

So I identified with Manning very strongly right away, in particular because of his statement that he was prepared to go to prison for life and even be executed to get this information out. That was the state of mind I was in forty years ago and I haven't heard it expressed by anybody in those forty years until now. So I've been waiting for someone to make what seemed to me an appropriate judgment that it was worth a great personal sacrifice in order to save lives and shorten a war.

Official Response to the Video

BWB: When the video first came out, it sparked outrage all over the world. Unfortunately, in this country most of the outrage, at least as reported by the corporate media, seemed to be about the leak itself rather than about the content of the video.

DE: Is that true with respect to the video? It's been true with respect to these later releases. Was it true that the video was strongly condemned for having been exposed?

BWB: It seems to me that what happened was the public relations machine of the Pentagon and the government tried to shift attention from the content of the video to the fact that this was an "illegal act" by a soldier.

DE: Okay, maybe. It seemed to me that the criticism was more toward what's the context here—asking whether the video itself was misleading. For example, was there an RPG there or not? There was an assertion that there was an RPG. In other words, saying that the video wasn't what it appeared to be. Those are fair enough to raise as questions, but it seemed to me that the questions were answered pretty well.

BWB: As far as I know, there hasn't been any further investigation of that event. Do you know of any official investigation regarding what happened in the helicopter that day?

DE: Actually, I think the military claims that they had investigated and concluded that the men were acting appropriately under the rules of engagement given what they feared or assumed. That may well be true, and of course that makes the thing even more ominous. Because it supports the assertion by Josh Stieber and Ethan McCord. Stieber, I recall, was the one who was in the same…

BWB: He was in the same unit.

DE: And McCord…

BWB: He was on the ground.

DE: He actually saved the child.

BWB: Right, exactly.

DE: Both of them said that this was an everyday kind of occurrence. This was a pattern and system that did reflect the rules of engagement, which obviously do permit enormous civilian death. [See "An Open Letter of Reconciliation and Responsibility to the Iraqi People" by Josh Stieber and Ethan McCord on page 213.]

BWB: One would have thought, or one would have hoped, I suppose, that outside the Pentagon itself there might have been some examination by the Congress about rules of engagement and if in fact this is deemed to be normal and acceptable one would have hoped for some kind of change in those rules.

DE: You could hope, but it's unrealistic to have a very high expectation. That's the kind of "second guessing," that monitoring and accountability and investigation, that Congress has always been very unwilling to do with respect to military operations. Not only Congress but the press and the public at large are willing to give very great leeway and benefit of the doubt to the troops on the ground perhaps in part out of some feeling of guilt for having sent them over there and not being under risk oneself. Nobody wants to be in a position of appearing to be critical or judgmental about the actions of men who are under fire themselves. And the effect of that, that's an understandable situation, but the effect is that the people who should be monitoring these matters actually are derelict. They do fail, they shirk that duty, they don't want to be in that position and, by the way, that's not only at the level of the troops, that goes up to the mid-level of the division commanders and the military, the Joint Chiefs of Staff. Civilians are on the whole extremely reluctant to criticize. Well, the military don't criticize themselves very effectively either. So what it means is that the enforcement of laws of war is very haphazard at best and very occasional and in general they aren't monitored. And the effect of that is they're flouted very widely.

The Motivation of Whistleblowers

BWB: Let's talk about Bradley Manning. You said you identified with him. Can you imagine what he is going through right now? He's in the brig in Quantico, Virginia, awaiting prosecution. You said that he had stated that he was ready to spend the rest of his life in prison or even face the death penalty in order to expose these acts of the U.S. military. So now he's in the brig. I think you've had some contact with him.

DE: I've spoken several times to his aunt who is his closest relative emotionally, supportively: Debra Van Alstyne, who is herself a lawyer, but not in this kind of law. She's totally loving to Bradley and she's seen him several times in jail. She said that he was in surprisingly good spirits. And he is aware of the amount of support that he's getting and very appreciative of it. He was very happy to hear that Michael Moore had expressed support of him, and that I had; and that it makes him feel a lot better.

But earlier, I think for more than a month, he was incommunicado in Kuwait where he didn't get any news of the outside world whatever and I think was pretty much in isolation. His aunt felt that he had not been in good spirits then, that he was pretty depressed. Even earlier we know from the Adrian Lamo reports that he wanted to find out what the reaction had been to the Apache helicopter video. He was concerned about that and I understand that really well. When you take the kinds of risks that he's facing, which are very heavy in his case, you certainly want to feel that at least people have had a chance to see and react to what you've put out and that it hasn't simply gotten buried.

BWB: You of all people can speak about the motivation of a person risking the rest of his or her life in prison to make classified information public. Can you talk a little bit more about that motivation? It seems an act of enormous courage to be able to do that.

DE: Well, let me first mention that Bradley is facing a very high likelihood of a very long sentence, quite possibly a life sentence. [Editor's note: New charges against Manning filed since this interview took place carry the death penalty.] He's under military law, which, as I now understand it, is significantly different from what he'd face in a civilian court. So his chance of being acquitted, except possibly on psychological grounds, is very low, because if you simply break a rule in the military, that has the status of a law. A directive from the president is in effect law for members of the armed services. That's not true for civilian subordinates. The president can't make criminal laws for civilians. But, in effect, he can for the military under the Universal Code of Military Justice.

So Bradley is facing the very real possibility of a life sentence not just from what has come out so far but also if other material comes out for which he gets blamed. Now, in my case, I, too, expected a life sentence if they prosecuted, which I thought they almost surely would. I expected to be found out. I don't know if Bradley did. He knew it was a risk or he wouldn't have been talking about prison. But he may not have had a high expectation. In my case, I did expect to be prosecuted and I expected something like a life sentence. In fact, I faced twelve felony counts which added up to a possible 115-year sentence, so that would amount to life even with time credited for good behavior.

BWB: What motivates you to do something like that?

DE: First of all, the stakes of possibly shortening a war even by a brief period would seem rather naturally to be worth one's life if anything is. Are there things for which one would give one's life? Most people can think of things—their children's well-being if they were threatened comes to mind. In the military, of course, you're trained and expected to risk or even give your life almost routinely in a combat situation. And, in fact, people live up to that. I've been in combat, as a civilian actually, but taking the same risks, and everywhere around me I saw people acting very courageously in what you could say was almost a routine unthinking response to a situation but not entirely unthinking or impulsive either. They were entering into situations that were clearly dangerous and were doing it quite willingly. So that's something we expect of our armed forces.

It seems almost strange to me that when these same people, in some cases, put on civilian clothes and work for the government, they act as if they're not willing to take any risk whatever—risking their clearance, their access, their role, their job. It would seem natural to apply the same standards that you do in combat. When you're dealing with matters of war and peace that involve possibly many, many lives, either losing them or saving them, you should be willing to take some risk, to pay a cost to stop a wrongful war. Yet most people don't seem willing to do that at all. They don't seem willing to take any risk at all. Given the personal stakes of losing your job or your clearance and possibly your marriage, it's not surprising that most people shy away from doing it. But why does virtually everyone? Why does almost nobody take that risk? That puzzles me. I don't have a real answer to it. Why is Bradley Manning almost unique? I'm sorry about that. I would like to change that frame of mind that prevents most people from taking that kind of risk to help stop a war and I think that publicizing what Bradley has done and, in general, the benefits of whistle-blowing, I think, might actually get more people to consider it and we would see more of it.

BWB: Well, there certainly are plenty of people within the military who had access to all of the same kind of information that Bradley Manning had.

DE: Oh, yes, the kind of thing he had access to—there must be at least hundreds, maybe more, who had the same access. So the real question is, why didn't any of them do it, too?

BWB: He hasn't so far been charged with the leak of all those other documents that have subsequently been posted by WikiLeaks.

DE: I think not. I think they've charged him with downloading those documents onto his computer. Apparently they haven't yet been able to prove that he passed them along to WikiLeaks. But in the military they can get him just for downloading, just for breaking the rules.

BWB: You say that the motivation, which is a powerful motivation, for you and for whoever leaked, the video and all the other documents was to be able to shorten or end the war.

DE: Shorten the war and save lives. In other cases of whistle-blowing we could point to, the stakes would be preserving the Constitution, exposing massive illegality, as in the case of the warrantless wiretapping being done by the National Security Agency, a major undermining of democracy I would say. So with stakes like that it seems it should be not only natural but really obligatory that people at least consider exposing that information even at very great personal cost and risk.

I guess the way to sum this up is when you talk about motivation in personal terms the stakes are high, the risk of doing it is quite high personally. But on the other hand the risks of not doing it for the society and for people's lives or for the Constitution are very high also. So you have a very strong motive to do it and a very strong motive not to do it—a strong personal motive. Those motives conflict, and what surprises me is how almost universally the personal concerns prevail. It seems to me that shouldn't happen nearly as universally as it does.

The Personal Price of Whistleblowing

BWB: I remember in a talk of yours I heard, you mentioned that you had talked to Mordechai Vanunu, who exposed Israel's nuclear weapons program and served years in jail, much of it in solitary confinement. Although he's out of jail now, he continues to be harassed by the Israeli government.

DE: He's had the worst you could have—eleven and a half years in solitary confinement, the kind of thing that Bradley had for a month or two in Kuwait. [Editor's note: Bradley Manning has been held in extreme isolation in the brig in Quantico, under conditions that Amnesty International and others have called "torture."] He had it for eleven and a half years, plus six and a half or so other years in a general prison population, and then was sent back to jail for months just recently, just last year, for violating what should be seen as illegal regulations which confine his movements and who he speaks to even after he's gotten out of prison. But he's always said that he's never regretted what he's done, though I think it came at times close to driving him crazy, paranoid, which fortunately he's recovered from once he got out. But the intent was to drive him crazy and it had considerable effect.

And it's not only Vanunu. Various whistle-blowers, none of whom have paid as heavy a price as Vanunu did or Manning probably will do, but who nevertheless have all paid very high prices—several years in prison, loss of marriages, loss or tremendous curtailing of their income for life even for those who didn't go to prison. I don't know any of them who have regretted what they did. They may have felt to some extent that they wished they hadn't been in a situation where exposing secrets was the right thing to do, but given that they were in that situation and were exposed to those guilty truths, they did feel that they had done the right thing and they were glad that they'd done it. And I expect that will be true of Manning.

The Effect on the Wars

BWB: It's too soon obviously for us to know whether the release of the video and these other documents will in fact shorten or end the war.

DE: Let me make a point about that, too. It has often been said of me, wrongly, that I was sure that what I was doing had a high likelihood of ending the war. That was never true. It was simply wrong. I always hoped that, at the most, it might have some chance of helping to bring an end to the war. I'm sure that's true of Manning and of Vanunu, too.

Now, the truth is that Vanunu's revelations, which put him in prison for eighteen years, had no effect at all as one can see. There's never been any effect on Israeli policy or anything else. So when I say he doesn't regret it, it's not because it achieved a lot, but because he felt it was clearly the right thing to do.

Manning's revelations may well have no effect, and I don't think that's the critical question when it comes to his own evaluation of whether he did the right thing or not. Similarly, in my case, we got a lot of attention for the Pentagon Papers, but what effect on policy? The Pentagon Papers themselves, their release, had no effect on Nixon's policy. He went right ahead with his secret planning to try to win the war. And the war got larger. It not only continued but it got larger after the Pentagon Papers came out. And I was well aware of that. In my case, I was part of a chain of events that *did* help shorten the war because they led to Nixon's resignation and that was crucial to the war's end, which came some nine months later. But that was because of Nixon having taken criminal action against me and not because of the Pentagon Papers. He had reasonable fears that I would release documents and other information about his own Vietnam policy. So Nixon's concerns about what else I would reveal led him to take criminal actions against me. And that in turn was a key factor in the impeachment proceedings that led to his resignation when those criminal actions were exposed.

So there was a lot of luck involved, and other people's contributions. A lot of people had to take various action, and some of them at some risk, to be part of this same chain of events. For example, Butterfield had to expose the taping, and Dean had to tell the prosecutors about the White House's break-in to my former psychiatrist's office. I could name a dozen people whose contribution was essential to this process of getting Nixon out of office, but my own actions, which led to Nixon's fears of me after I was indicted, were also essential. They were part of that process.

Now, there could very well be an analogy here. On the one hand, they have Manning in custody so they can control his actions. But they don't yet have Assange in custody and I'm pretty sure that they are doing many things, some of them illegal I would guess, against Assange right now to try to keep him from making further revelations, some of which might come from Bradley Manning. So that process is not over yet. It could well be that some of those criminal actions might get exposed, and if exposed would jeopardize the policy or would put the Obama administration in trouble. Actually, that's less likely than it was in my day. Some of the actions they took against me forty years ago were clearly illegal then and some of them still are. But many of them have become legal or have become accepted. So the president is not as much at risk even if it comes to assassinating Assange, which several people have called for explicitly—columnists and congressmen. I saw a column with a headline, "Why is Assange still alive?"

Actually, there's a good deal of acceptance of such a move at this point, where it's known that the president has named various people, including Anwar al-Awlaki, as an enemy combatant, as someone who can be assassinated right now. And he could make that ruling against Assange. That would not be surprising. Forty years ago, I think that would have put him in danger of impeachment. It doesn't now. There isn't that much protest against this assassination policy.

So things have changed, and yet, to an act of truth telling can set in motion ripples of events that even after months and years can have an effect that was not foreseeable in the beginning. Conceivably, some of those effects could be bad. Don't rule that out. But they could have some very good effects that you don't see for a long time.

The WikiLeaks Phenomenon

BWB: Can you reflect for a minute or so on the phenomenon of WikiLeaks. Would we have all of this happening if it weren't for WikiLeaks? And why do we need a WikiLeaks?

DE: Well, it's clear that this administration is going after whistleblowers. I was the first person to be prosecuted for a leak. Ford prosecuted one, and George W. Bush prosecuted three people in connection with the AIPAC [American Israel Public Affairs Committee] leaks, although that prosecution was subsequently dropped by Obama. Obama has himself initiated three prosecutions: Thomas Drake, who's being prosecuted now for leaking information from the NSA [National Security Administration]; Shamai Leibowitz, who pled guilty to leaking FBI documents and who's in prison now; and Bradley Manning. So, clearly, Obama is willing to take legal action and to use a very dubious law—the Espionage Act—in this connection. The Espionage Act was not intended to be used for prosecuting whistleblowers when it was passed and has a very questionable constitutional basis if it is used for that reason. That's what's kept other presidents from using it more than a very few times in the forty years since I was the first— or in all years before that when there were no prosecutions at all.

So there is a willingness to prosecute. The risks are higher for being identified as a leaker than they were before, even under George W. Bush. In that context there's a greater need for WikiLeaks than there ever was, and an increasing need, because WikiLeaks offers a greater prospect of being able to leak especially large amounts of material anonymously. Of course, without the Internet, without the digital technology, you couldn't have leaked that amount anyway, physically there'd be really no way to do it. I couldn't have done that forty years ago. Now you can put out a large amount of material and if you use WikiLeaks—and maybe there will be some other sites that will come up and will offer the same possibility of doing it anonymously. The reason that Manning was identified apparently was that for some reason that we don't know yet he chose to describe what he'd done in some detail to a guy who in turn informed on him. But that wasn't WikiLeaks's fault.

BWB: WikiLeaks really made it possible. The corporate media today is less likely to be a site for this kind of information until it's exposed in another way.

DE: That's what I'm saying, and moreover, things will get worse in that respect. I think that it's quite likely that the incoming Republican Congress will pass an Official Secrets Act, which will clearly criminalize the kind of thing that I did or that Bradley Manning did. Whereas, as I've been saying, it's not clearly criminal under existing law, including the Espionage Act. But if they pass an Official Secrets Act, which is clearly intended to criminalize the release of any classified data—and we do not have such an act now—if they pass that, then I think the flow of leaks will diminish very sharply. There still will be some disclosures—I myself thought that there was an Official Secrets Act when I put out the documents and it didn't stop me. And it will not stop people like Bradley. But unfortunately there aren't too many people like Bradley.

So it will stop most and that will mean we will just rely on government handouts which basically means we've given up democracy, the ability to hold officials accountable, to replace them, to understand what they're doing and to have any real influence on their policy. I think an effective Official Secrets Act goes very far toward diminishing our ability to be a democracy in the field of foreign affairs.

BWB: Well, Dan, thank you very much for giving us your time today to share with us your thoughts about these important matters. We're grateful to have the benefit of your experience and insight.

DE: Glad to help.

November 19, 2010

An Open Letter of Reconciliation and Responsibility to the Iraqi People

from Current and Former Members of the U.S. Military

In July of 2007, Josh Stieber and Ethan McCord were members of the Army's Bravo Company 2-16, the unit involved in the massacre depicted in the leaked Collateral Murder *video. McCord was the soldier who pulled the injured Iraqi children from the shot-up van. Soon after the release of the video, Stieber and McCord wrote the following letter of apology to the people of Iraq.*

Peace be with you.

To all of those who were injured or lost loved ones during the July 2007 Baghdad shootings depicted in the *Collateral Murder* Wikileaks video:

We write to you, your family, and your community with awareness that our words and actions can never restore your losses.

We are both soldiers who occupied your neighborhood for fourteen months. Ethan McCord pulled your daughter and son from the van, and when doing so, saw the faces of his own children back home. Josh Stieber was in the same company but was not there that day, though he contributed to your pain, and the pain of your community on many other occasions.

There is no bringing back all that was lost. What we seek is to learn from our mistakes and do everything we can to tell others of our experiences and how the people of the United States need to realize what we have done and are doing to you and the people of your country. We humbly ask you what we can do to begin to repair the damage we caused.

We have been speaking to whoever will listen, telling them that what was shown in the WikiLeaks video only begins to depict the suffering we have created. From our own experiences, and the experiences of other veterans we have talked to, we know that the acts depicted in this video are everyday occurrences of this war: this is the nature of how U.S.-led wars are carried out in this region.

We acknowledge our part in the deaths and injuries of your loved ones as we tell Americans what we were trained to do and what we carried out in the name of "God and country." The soldier in the video said that your husband shouldn't have brought your children to battle, but we are acknowledging our responsibility for bringing the battle to your neighborhood, and to your family. We did unto you what we would not want done to us.

More and more Americans are taking responsibility for what was done in our name. Though we have acted with cold hearts far too many times, we have not forgotten our actions towards you. Our heavy hearts still hold hope that we can restore inside our country the acknowledgment of your humanity that we were taught to deny.

Our government may ignore you, concerned more with its public image. It has also ignored many veterans who have returned physically injured or mentally troubled by what they saw and did in your country. But the time is long overdue that we say that the value of our nation's leaders no longer represent us. Our Secretary of Defense may say the U.S. won't lose its reputation over this, but we stand and say that our reputation's importance pales in comparison to our common humanity.

We have asked our fellow veterans and service-members, as well as civilians both in the United States and abroad, to sign in support of this letter, and to offer their names as a testimony to our common humanity, to distance ourselves from the destructive policies of our nation's leaders, and to extend our hands to you.

With such pain, friendship might be too much to ask. Please accept our apology, our sorrow, our care, and our dedication to change from the inside out. We are doing what we can to speak out against the wars and military policies responsible for what happened to you and your loved ones. Our hearts are open to hearing how we can take any steps to support you through the pain that we have caused.

Solemnly and Sincerely,

Josh Stieber, former specialist, U.S. Army

Ethan McCord, former specialist, U.S. Army

This letter was originally published by Iraq Veterans Against the War, on April 15, 2010. Since its publication, Josh and Ethan have become involved in reparations and reconciliation efforts, working with the group Iraqi Health Now to provide direct aid to people in Iraq living under occupation. The IVAW Reparations Committee continues to build and grow. U.S. Labor Against the War (USLAW) and IVAW do solidarity work with Iraqi trade unions organizing for their rights while living under occupation. This included an IVAW/USLAW delegation to the first Iraqi Trade Union Conference in March 2009 to build relationships and unity in the struggle.

Afterword

★ ★ ★ ★ ★

Operation Recovery

"I am just trying to get help," insisted Jeff Hanks, active-duty U.S. Army infantryman, who has served in Iraq and Afghanistan. "My goal in this situation is to simply heal. And they wonder why there are so many suicides." Jeff spoke rapidly over the phone from Virginia, where he, his wife, and his two young daughters are staying while he is AWOL from the military. Days earlier, Jeff had walked out of an airport, refusing to board a plane headed for Kuwait, which was to be his first stop on his way back to Afghanistan.

During his mid-September leave from his second combat tour with the 101st Airborne Division, Jeff sought help from Fort Bragg and Fort Campbell military doctors for PTSD and physical wounds sustained in battle. Yet, just as his treatment was getting started, his command interfered, insisting that his military health care providers grant him clearance for immediate deployment. His providers acquiesced, even though they had not completed preliminary testing.

Jeff, who has trouble being in large crowds of people and difficulty controlling his anger, says he is in no state to deploy back to the war from which he is still struggling to heal. The thirty-year-old soldier decided that his only choice was to go AWOL. Jeff plans to turn himself into his command at Fort Campbell on Veterans Day, November 11. He will be accompanied by supporters, including members of Iraq Veterans Against the War.

As the war in Afghanistan stretches into its tenth year, now the longest war in U.S. history, Jeff's story has become all too familiar in a military that is overextended and exhausted, pushing soldiers beyond their mental and physical capacities in order to fill the ranks. The wars in Iraq and Afghanistan have been marked by staggering rates of trauma and suicide. Between 20 percent and 50 percent of all service members deployed to Iraq and Afghanistan have suffered PTSD.[1] Suicide rates among active-duty service members are twice as high as that of the civilian population and veterans with PTSD are six times more likely to attempt suicide.[2]

In response to these developments, Iraq Veterans Against the War have launched a campaign—Operation Recovery— calling for an end to the deployment of traumatized troops. This two-thousand-strong organization, comprising veterans and active-duty troops who have served since September 11, 2001, insists that Jeff's situation is not isolated, but rather, has become endemic to the current wars in Iraq and Afghanistan. "Many troops currently deployed to combat theater suffer from Post-Traumatic Stress Disorder, Traumatic Brain Injury [TBI] and Military Sexual Trauma," says Jason Hurd, a former soldier who served in Iraq and is active in the Operation Recovery Campaign. "We find this situation unacceptable and demand an end to these inhumane deployments."

---

1   Karen H. Seal, et al., "Getting Beyond 'Don't Ask; Don't Tell': An Evaluation of U.S. Veterans Administration Postdeployment Mental Health Screening of Veterans Returning from Iraq and Afghanistan," *American Journal of Public Health* 98 (2008): 714–720. See also "Comparisons of PTSD Rates," *Journal of Traumatic Stress* 23, no. 1 (February 2010).

2   Department of Veterans' Affairs, "Suicide and PTSD"; Armen Keteyian, "Suicide Epidemic Among Veterans," CBSNews.com, November 13, 2007, http://www.cbsnews.com/stories/2007/11/13/cbsnews_investigates/main3496471.shtml; Mark Thompson "Invisible Wounds: Mental Health and the Military," CNN, August 22, 2010, http://www.time.com/time/magazine/article/0,9171,2008886,00.html.

Mental and Physical Wounds

Jeff, who grew up in Beebe, Arkansas, deployed to Iraq in 2008, a tour that eventually earned him a Combat Infantry Badge. During his time in Iraq, Jeff saw "the most brutal things of any of his deployments," he says. "It really bothered me. I think about it all the time." Jeff's Iraq deployment was marked by stressful combat patrols that kept him "always on edge." In 2008, he was witness to the aftermath of a car bomb explosion in a crowded marketplace in Balad, Iraq. It resulted in what he describes as "mass casualties." He saw one little girl, the age of his oldest daughter at the time, who had been gravely injured by the bomb, but still alive. "I can still see that little girl," he says. "I dream about her to this day."

Jeff says that he and others in his unit were not given adequate care for the mental wounds they sustained in battle, with mental health professionals only coming for short visits once a month. He describes his only experience seeing a therapist in Iraq: "It was a total joke," he says. "The guy just sat there and wrote stuff down and nothing ever came of it."

Jeff tells of one person in his unit who developed a severe drinking problem during his tour. "I know it stemmed from stuff he saw in Iraq," says Jeff. "The command never pursued mental counseling of any kind for him. They told us not to speak to him and they eventually just kicked him out. He probably didn't get disability pay or anything."

"When I came home from Iraq I changed a lot. I noticed I had a lot of anger problems and I couldn't sleep," says Jeff. Family and friends noticed as well, and Jeff's coldness and distance began to eat away at his marriage, says his wife Christina. "When he came back from Iraq, he would look at me so cold. There was nothing in his eyes. That was the thing that bothered me the most. He was so unlike himself. The old Jeff used to joke around, he used to go out and socialize." The couple separated and Christina was left alone to raise their two daughters.

Jeff says that, back at the Fort Campbell, Kentucky, base where he was stationed, suicide was a widespread problem among the 101st Airborne Division. "There were multiple suicide attempts on base in Kentucky. For a while, we were having people kill themselves every other day," says Jeff.

After serving in Iraq, Jeff was deployed to Afghanistan on May 3 of this year. "In Afghanistan, there is more of a constant threat than there is in Iraq," says Jeff, describing a deployment defined by constant mortar attacks, unclear missions, and low morale among U.S. soldiers. "We had no clear mission and nothing got done. We basically just sat in a valley waiting to get hit," he says. In one incident, five U.S. soldiers were hit by a roadside bomb. "One died for sure and I don't know about the rest," says Jeff. "We had to sit on base and wait for them to be stabilized. We heard them screaming. It stuck with me. You can never get rid of that sound."

Jeff says that, as in Iraq, medical treatment in Afghanistan was scarce and inadequate. "Combat stress people hardly ever came to the base. And it is hard to talk in a situation like that, since you are still in the war and on edge all the time," he says. On top of limited resources, people in Jeff's unit were teased and belittled when they asked for mental or physical health care. One private, who was blown back into a building after a mortar attack, complained of headaches and nausea to his command. "He was made fun of by the command in front of everybody," he says. "There is a saying in the military: 'What, you got sand in your vagina?'" Jeff is certain that this dissuaded many who needed care from seeking it. "It keeps you from seeking help. I didn't seek help. I wanted to, but I would be ostracized."

Three weeks before going on leave from Afghanistan, a mortar went off near Jeff, blowing him up against a wall. He still suffers severe headaches from the incident.

Coming Home

When he went on leave from Afghanistan in mid-September, Jeff began to notice how profoundly he had been affected by his combat experience. He describes being seized with uncontrollable anger, having panic attacks at the slightest stimuli and being unable to relate to his family and loved ones.

Having reconciled with his wife Christina, he had been looking forward to spending time with her and the kids. "I had been so excited to see my family when I came home on leave," he says. "But when I was actually around them, they were just completely overwhelming."

"My daughters see how much Jeff has changed," says Christina. My older one says that Daddy is not as nice as he used to be. She says, 'I don't like Daddy anymore.'"

In one incident, when Jeff and Christina were shopping at Wal-Mart, Jeff was temporarily left alone when his wife went browsing in a different aisle. "I freaked out. There were too many people around me. I couldn't be left alone." Christina says she returned to find Jeff frantically insisting that they leave immediately.

Jeff tells of being afraid to sleep in the same bed as his wife, concerned that he would attack her in his sleep.

One day, Jeff was overwhelmed with anger when a police officer "copped an attitude" toward his dad who had asked the officer for directions to a baseball game. "It triggered something in me," says Jeff. "I really wanted to hurt him."

"His mother has called me many times in tears about this," says Christina. "She knows her son and she knows he is different."

Jeff became concerned about whether he was fit for his imminent deployment. "If you have trouble controlling your anger at home, what are you going to do when you are in a situation holding a loaded weapon?" he asks.

In the Raleigh, North Carolina, airport where he was to catch a plane to Kuwait, Jeff had a panic attack in response to a stranger loudly clapping his hands. "I freaked out and was just like, I gotta go. I can't do this," he says. Jeff walked out of the airport and checked himself into the Fort Bragg Emergency Room, the nearest military hospital.

Jeff was told by Fort Bragg doctors that they could not diagnose anything beyond the airport panic attack, because he was based out of Fort Campbell. Jeff arranged to meet his Fort Campbell command, where he was listed as AWOL for failing to board his plane. At Fort Campbell, he was passed around to various social workers, who eventually scheduled him an appointment with a mental health care doctor for Monday morning, October 11, at the Fort Campbell Medical Center. However, the Thursday before the appointment was to take place, Jeff's sergeant called him and said he needed to get immediate clearance to go back to Afghanistan that Friday, meaning he would never get to go to his scheduled appointment. Jeff later found out that his command called his doctors and order them to give him immediate clearance.

"I hadn't even been seen by a professional doctor," he says. "All I want is treatment. They were the ones who sent me over there. Now they won't even give me help when I need it." Jeff says he was determined to get help one way or another: "At that point, my only option was to leave."

Jeff has since been diagnosed by two civilian psychiatric professionals as having severe PTSD. He is currently weighing his options for meeting his urgent mental health care needs.

A Widespread Problem

"The redeployment of traumatized troops is a horrible problem," says Ethan McCord, a veteran whose unit was shown in the *Collateral Murder* video distributed by WikiLeaks. [see "An Open Letter of Reconciliation and Responsibility to the Iraqi People From Current and Former Members of the U.S. Military," on page 213.] "I was denied treatment for the mental and physical wounds I sustained in battle, like so many others."

"In multiple units across all branches we're seeing commanders order service members to the battlefield who just aren't serviceable," says Chantelle Bateman, a former Marine who served in Iraq. "Rather than repairing them, we are sacrificing their long term well-being, their immediate safety and that of the people they are serving with."

As the wars drag on, veterans are demanding an end to the overextension and redeployment of wounded soldiers. On October 7, the ninth anniversary of the Afghanistan war, dozens of Iraq and Afghanistan veterans marched from Walter Reed Medical Center to Capitol Hill in Washington, D.C., to announce Operation Recovery. A campaign statement reads: "While we recognize that we must stop the deployment of all soldiers in order to end the occupations in Iraq and Afghanistan, we see the deployment of soldiers with Post Traumatic Stress Disorder, Traumatic Brain Injuries and Military Sexual Trauma as particularly cruel, inhumane and dangerous. Military commanders across all branches are pushing service members far past human limits for the sake of 'combat readiness.' We cannot allow those commanders to continue to ignore the welfare of their troops who are, after all, human beings."

According to the Department of Defense (DOD), even if a military medical professional deems a service member unfit to deploy, a commanding officer can waive medical evaluation and order the service member into combat.[3] While the DOD is not forthcoming about the rate at which this occurs, high rates of PTSD and multiple deployments suggest that cases like Jeff's are common. Almost 30 percent of troops on their third deployment suffer severe mental health problems. By 2008, nearly 33 percent of troops had served two tours to Iraq or Afghanistan, while 10 percent had served three tours, trends that can only increase as the war in Afghanistan reaches its tenth year. Today, over eleven thousand troops have served six tours, with each tour greatly increasing a service member's chances of developing mental health problems, including PTSD, TBI and combat stress, as well as Military Sexual Trauma, caused by rape and sexual assault from within the ranks.[4]

Top military brass acknowledge that suicides and violent crimes plague the military, with four combat veterans recently killing themselves at Fort Hood, Texas, in one week, one of them a suspected murder-suicide still under investigation. "The emergency issue for me right now is the suicide issue," said Adm. Mike Mullen, chairman of the Joint Chiefs of Staff, the highest-ranking person in the U.S. armed forces.

---

3   DDI 1332.14(8)c Updated March 29, 2010.
4   The Alaska Army National Guard, "A Tremendous Shortfall: Report of the Veterans For America National Guard Program," October 15, 2008; Mark Thompson, "America's Medicated Army," *Time*, June 5, 2008.

The recently exposed kill team in Afghanistan, in which U.S. troops hunted, killed, and mutilated Afghan civilians, collecting their body parts as trophies, involved at least one soldier who was on a cocktail of medications for TBI.

"They are sending troops right back into the situation that traumatized them before they have the time to heal," says McCord. It's ruining our youth in the military. Operation Recovery is trying to stop this."

Jeff Hanks remains determined to get the mental and physical health care he needs and is working with the Operation Recovery team of Iraq Veterans Against the War and Courage to Resist to figure out how to meet his immediate health care needs. "Five to ten years from now, these people are not going to care about me. I don't want to be a basket case. I don't want to go to a school play of my kid's and freak out in a big crowd," he says. "I just want help and they want to send me back to war instead of helping me."

—Sarah Lazare

This article first appeared at Truthout.org on November 5, 2010.

Supporting GI Resistance

Every day, GIs decide they no longer want to participate in the inhumane life of the military. As civilians, we have opportunities to support these courageous soldiers. Almost every soldier who considers resisting feels isolated, scared, and alone. We can show them that there is a growing community who stand with them in their refusal to participate.

When my son finished Basic and AIT and decided he wanted to get out of the military, I was grateful that I worked with Courage to Resist and could guide him toward the resources he needed. By contacting the GI Rights Hotline, he was referred to a civilian psychologist who later referred him to a GI rights attorney who negotiated his release.

When you close this book, we hope you will join us by becoming involved in the following organizations. Each of these offers concrete support to members of the military who need information about their choices, physical and emotional care, and ways to find financial help. If you know people who are in the military, please refer them to these groups so that they have the resources they need.

Courage to Resist
www.couragetoresist.org
Courage to Resist provides political, emotional, and material support to all military objectors critical of our government's current policies of empire. As a grassroots project with limited resources, Courage to Resist nevertheless has a record of successfully working with many resisters and their families in raising the needed funds for civilian legal representation as well as public education campaigns. Courage to Resist makes a special effort to work with resisters to tell their stories, in their own words and from their own unique perspectives.

Iraq Veterans Against the War
www.ivaw.org
Iraq Veterans Against the War (IVAW) was founded by Iraq veterans in July 2004 at the annual convention of Veterans for Peace (VFP) in Boston, to give a voice to the large number of active-duty service people and veterans who are against this war, but are under various pressures to remain silent. IVAW members educate the public about the realities of the Iraq War by speaking in communities and to the media about their experiences. Members also dialogue with youth in classrooms about the realities of military service. IVAW supports all those resisting the war, including conscientious objectors and others facing military prosecution for their refusal to fight. IVAW's current campaign, Operation Recovery, is the focus of the article on page "Operation Recovery" on page 219 of this book.

The GI Rights Hotline

(877-447-4487)

www.girightshotline.org

Since 1994, the GI Rights Hotline has been providing free, confidential, and accurate information on U.S. military regulations and practices to service members, veterans, potential recruits, and their families including information on military discharges, AWOL, UA, and GI rights. The hotline is a consortium of more than twenty nongovernmental, nonprofit organizations located in more than fifteen states and in Germany. Some of the counselors are veterans, some are lawyers and some have decades of military counseling experience. The counselors provide resources and counseling options.

War Resisters League

www.warresistersleague.org

The oldest secular pacifist organization in the United States, the War Resisters League has been resisting war at home and war abroad since 1923. Their work for nonviolent revolution has spanned decades and has been shaped by the new visions and strategies of each generation's peacemakers. They believe that there are interwoven systems of domination and exploitation at the roots of inequality and injustice, and that to remove all causes of war, we must collaborate and stand in solidarity with oppressed people across the globe. WRL is committed to building a broad-based movement against war in all its forms.

Civilian-Soldier Alliance

www.civsol.org

Founded in 2007, the Civilian-Soldier Alliance is an organization of civilians working with veterans and active-duty service-members to build a GI resistance movement toward a just foreign policy. They work with and support service-members and veterans to withdraw military support from the occupations of Iraq and Afghanistan, supporting resistance within the military that empowers service members to have a voice and develop as leaders organizing for change. To help build this GI-led movement, they work with fellow civilians to build a reliable, committed, and experienced support structure for military personnel. They believe that organizing to withdraw military support from the war can not only win tangible victories, but can also be a transformative process whereby vets and civilians develop the skills and confidence necessary to organize for long-term change.

We also encourage you to get involved with local peace and antiwar groups. In addition, you can work with organizations led by and in support of Afghans, Iraqis, and other Arab communities including Palestinians, and all those directly affected by war and occupation. Such groups as the Revolutionary Association of Women in Afghanistan (RAWA) and the Arab Resource Organizing Center play an important role in building power in opposition to U.S. imperialism. Our movements are stronger more effective and more just when we build solidarity across deep divides and work hand in hand with Iraqi and Afghan struggles for justice and peace. By supporting individual resisters and these organizations, you will also step into a community working to end the policies of empire and build participatory democracy.

—*Cynthia Whitman-Bradley*

About the Editors

Buff Whitman-Bradley

Buff Whitman-Bradley, a long-time peace and social justice activist, has been working with Courage to Resist since 2003. He has been a member of the CtR organizing collective, and was the originator and producer of the Courage to Resist Audio Project. He is also a member of ¡Presente! a nonviolent direct action affinity group actively opposing war and empire. He has worked for many years as a professional writer and editor, authored and edited educational books and materials, nonfiction books for children, and books of poetry. He has coproduced and directed two documentary films, *Por Que Venimos*, and with his partner Cynthia, an award-winning documentary about visitors to death row, *Outside In*.

Sarah Lazare

Sarah Lazare is a writer and organizer in the U.S. antiwar and GI resistance movement, as a member of The Civilian-Soldier Alliance and Courage to Resist. She is also a coorganizer of the "Dialogues Against Militarism" U.S. war resister delegation to Palestine/Israel, to show support for Israeli youth refusing to join the military and Palestinians resisting occupation. Sarah is active in economic and social justice organizing in the U.S. and seeks to connect domestic struggles for justice and liberation with global movements against U.S. war and empire. She is also an independent journalist, writing articles for publications ranging from the *Nation* to Truthout.org to *Al Jazeera English*.

Cynthia Whitman-Bradley

Cynthia Whitman-Bradley has been a member of Courage to Resist since 2003 and served on the organizing collective from 2003 to 2009. As one of the members of the affinity group ¡Presente!, she has participated in many direct actions to stop the wars in Afghanistan and Iraq. With her partner, Buff Whitman-Bradley, she coproduced the documentary *Outside In,* which tells the stories of those who visit condemned prisoners on California's death row. She is a former elementary school and preschool teacher and currently supports women during childbirth as a birth doula.

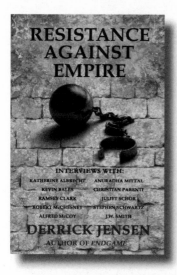

Resistance Against Empire

Interviewer/Editor: Derrick Jensen
$20.00
978-1-60486-046-7

A scathing indictment of U.S. domestic and foreign policy, this collection of interviews gathers incendiary insights from 10 of today's most experienced and knowledgeable activists. Whether it's Ramsey Clark describing the long history of military invasion, Alfred McCoy detailing the relationship between CIA activities and the increase in the global heroin trade, Stephen Schwartz reporting the obscene costs of nuclear armaments, or Katherine Albrecht tracing the horrors of the modern surveillance state, this investigation of global governance is sure to inform, engage, and incite readers.

Full list of Interviewees:

- Stephen Schwartz, author of *Atomic Audit: The Costs and Consequences of U.S. Nuclear Weapons*.
- Katherine Albrecht is the director of CASPIAN (Consumers Against Supermarket Privacy Invasion and Numbering).
- Robert McChesney is the author of seven books concerned with the contradiction between a for-profit corporate media and the communications requirements of a democratic society.
- J.W. Smith is the author of *The World's Wasted Wealth*.
- Juliet Schor is co-founder of the Center for a New American Dream
- Alfred McCoy is the author of *The Politics of Heroin in Southeast Asia* and winner of a Grant Goodman Prize.
- Christian Parenti is the author of *Lockdown America: Police and Prisons in the Age of Crisis*.
- Kevin Bales is an expert on modern slavery and is the author of *Disposable People: New Slavery in the Global Economy*.
- Ramsey Clark was Attorney General under Lyndon Johnson, playing an important role in the history of the Civil Rights movement and continuing on as unstinting critic of U.S. foreign policy.
- Anuradha Mittal is an internationally renowned expert on trade, development, human rights, democracy, and agriculture issues, and is the founder of The Oakland Institute, which works to ensure public participation and democratic debate on crucial economic and social policy issues.

War and Civil Disobedience CD
Howard Zinn
$14.95
978-1-60486-099-3

What are citizens to do when confronted by unjust laws and when their government embroils them in unjust wars?

Delivered in the context of the current U.S. war in Iraq, this is a scintillating lecture and discussion by the legendary teacher, historian, playwright, and activist. The efforts of Zinn to recover and pass on stories of civil disobedience to the unjust wars of U.S. history offers models, ideas, and inspirations for how and why we might go about challenging and changing the structures of power.

Iraq: The Forever War CD
Noam Chomsky
$14.95
978-1-60486-100-6

Presenting an arresting analysis of U.S. foreign policy and the war on terror, this original recording delivers a provocative lecture on the nation's past and present use of force. Demonstrating how imperial powers have historically invented fantastic reasons to sell their wars to their people, this powerful examination illustrates the attack on Iraq as not just a mistake but also a crime, proposing that the criminals behind it should be brought to justice. The discourse focuses on the present U.S. disregard for the Geneva Conventions and the dangerous and immoral use of "anticipatory self-defense" to undermine the United Nations Charter and international law.

In spite of this dark assessment, Chomsky maintains hope for democracy at home and abroad by inspiring listeners to shake off our political malaise and work to build a more egalitarian future for all.

Deserter DVD
Big Noise Films
$14.95
978-1-60486-012-2

Deserter is the journey of Ryan and Jen Johnson—a deserting soldier and his young wife—as they flee across the country to seek refugee status over the Canadian border. As they move from safe house to safe house, we get to know Ryan and Jen—two, shy, small-town kids from the Central Valley who joined the military because there were no jobs, and find they must make a heroic stand in order to escape an illegal and immoral war. *Deserter* is a political road movie with one of the few happy endings that this war has given us.

Special Feature:
Discussion with Amy Goodman and U.S. Army *Deserter* Ryan Johnson at the North American premiere of *Deserter*.

Awards and Festivals:

- Official Selection: International Documentary Festival of Amsterdam

- OVNI - Barcelona

- Singapore International Film Festival

- BeyondTV – UK

- MountainTop Human Rights Film Festival

About Big Noise Media:
Big Noise Tactical Media is a collective of media-makers dedicated to circulating beautiful, passionate, revolutionary images.

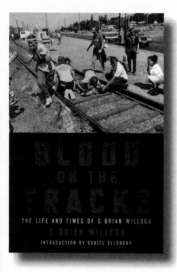

Blood on the Tracks: The Life and Times of S. Brian Willson

S. Brian Willson
Introduction: Daniel Ellsberg
$20.00
978-1-60486-421-2

"We are not worth more, they are not worth less." This is the mantra of S. Brian Willson and the theme that runs throughout his compelling psycho-historical memoir. Willson's story begins in small-town, rural America, where he grew up as a "Commie-hating, baseball-loving Baptist," moves through life-changing experiences in Viet Nam, Nicaragua and elsewhere, and culminates with his commitment to a localized, sustainable lifestyle.

In telling his story, Willson provides numerous examples of the types of personal, risk-taking, nonviolent actions he and others have taken in attempts to educate and effect political change: tax refusal, fasting, and obstruction tactics. It was such actions that thrust Brian Willson into the public eye in the mid-'80s, first as a participant in a high-profile, water-only "Veterans Fast for Life" against the Contra war being waged by his government in Nicaragua. Then, on a fateful day in September 1987, the world watched in horror as Willson was run over by a U.S. government munitions train during a nonviolent blocking action in which he expected to be removed from the tracks and arrested.

Throughout his personal journey Willson struggles with the question, "Why was it so easy for me, a 'good' man, to follow orders to travel 9,000 miles from home to participate in killing people who clearly were not a threat to me or any of my fellow citizens?" He eventually comes to the realization that the "American Way of Life" is AWOL from humanity, and that the only way to recover our humanity is by changing our consciousness, one individual at a time, while striving for collective cultural changes toward "less and local." Thus, Willson offers up his personal story as a metaphorical map for anyone who feels the need to be liberated from the American Way of Life—a guidebook for anyone called by conscience to question continued obedience to vertical power structures while longing to reconnect with the human archetypes of cooperation, equity, mutual respect and empathy.

FRIENDS OF

These are indisputably momentous times – the financial system is melting down globally and the Empire is stumbling. Now more than ever there is a vital need for radical ideas.

In the three years since its founding – and on a mere shoestring – PM Press has risen to the formidable challenge of publishing and distributing knowledge and entertainment for the struggles ahead. With over 100 releases to date, we have published an impressive and stimulating array of literature, art, music, politics, and culture. Using every available medium, we've succeeded in connecting those hungry for ideas and information to those putting them into practice.

Friends of PM allows you to directly help impact, amplify, and revitalize the discourse and actions of radical writers, filmmakers, and artists. It provides us with a stable foundation from which we can build upon our early successes and provides a much-needed subsidy for the materials that can't necessarily pay their own way. You can help make that happen – and receive every new title automatically delivered to your door once a month – by joining as a Friend of PM Press. And, we'll throw in a free T-Shirt when you sign up.

Here are your options:

- $25 a month: Get all books and pamphlets plus 50% discount on all webstore purchases
- $25 a month: Get all CDs and DVDs plus 50% discount on all webstore purchases
- $40 a month: Get all PM Press releases plus 50% discount on all webstore purchases
- $100 a month: Superstar - Everything plus PM merchandise, free downloads, and 50% discount on all webstore purchases

For those who can't afford $25 or more a month, we're introducing **Sustainer Rates** at $15, $10 and $5. Sustainers get a free PM Press t-shirt and a 50% discount on all purchases from our website.

Your Visa or Mastercard will be billed once a month, until you tell us to stop. Or until our efforts succeed in bringing the revolution around. Or the financial meltdown of Capital makes plastic redundant. Whichever comes first.

PM Press was founded at the end of 2007 by a small collection of folks with decades of publishing, media, and organizing experience. PM Press co-conspirators have published and distributed hundreds of books, pamphlets, CDs, and DVDs. Members of PM have founded enduring book fairs, spearheaded victorious tenant organizing campaigns, and worked closely with bookstores, academic conferences, and even rock bands to deliver political and challenging ideas to all walks of life. We're old enough to know what we're doing and young enough to know what's at stake.

We seek to create radical and stimulating fiction and non-fiction books, pamphlets, t-shirts, visual and audio materials to entertain, educate, and inspire you. We aim to distribute these through every available channel with every available technology, whether that means you are seeing anarchist classics at our bookfair stalls; reading our latest vegan cookbook at the café; downloading geeky fiction e-books; or digging new music and timely videos from our website.

PM Press is always on the lookout for talented and skilled volunteers, artists, activists and writers to work with. If you have a great idea for a project or can contribute in some way, please get in touch.

PM Press
PO Box 23912
Oakland CA 94623
510-658-3906
www.pmpress.org